10/03

Europe Rules the World

VOLUME 7

Europe Rules
the World

— | VOLUME 7 | —

Other titles in the World History by Era series:

WORLD HISTORY BY ERA

Europe Rules the World

VOLUME 7

Jeff Hay, *Book Editor*

Daniel Leone, *President*
Bonnie Szumski, *Publisher*
Scott Barbour, *Managing Editor*

Greenhaven Press, Inc., San Diego, California

Library of Congress Cataloging-in-Publication Data

Europe Rules the World / Jeff Hay, book editor.
    p. cm. — (World history by era; vol. 7)
   Includes bibliographical references and index.
   ISBN 0-7377-0766-6 (pbk. : alk. paper) —
ISBN 0-7377-0767-4 (lib. : alk. paper)
   1. History, Modern—19th century. 2. Civilization, Modern—19th century. 3. Europe—History—19th century. 4. Revolutions—History—20th century. 5. Imperialism. 6. Technology—History—19th century. I. Hay, Jeff. II. Series.

D358 .E87 2002
909.81—dc21   2001033511

CONTENTS

Chapter 1: An Era of Challenge and Transition

1. Thousands Race to California in Search of Gold

By Donald Barr Chidsey   36

As soon as word of the discovery of gold in California reached the American public the great gold rush of 1849 was underway.

2. The Domination of the Bourgeoisie

By Karl Marx and Friedrich Engels   40

Two founders of communism describe how Europe is dominated and corrupted by capitalists: factory owners, bankers, and large landowners.

3. Industry and Empire on Display: Britain's Crystal Palace Exhibition

By Asa Briggs   47

In 1851 Britain staged the first ever world's fair, for which they erected a great structure known as the Crystal Palace in London.

4. The Failed Taiping Rebellion in China

By John King Fairbank   51

Despite attracting the support of millions of people and taking command of huge territories, rebels fail to bring change to China.

5. Japan Is Opened to the West

By Richard Storry   56

Seeking trade rights and other privileges, American naval officers force Japan's isolationist Tokugawa shogunate to allow foreigners into the country.

Chapter 2: National Unity and Technological Change

T he late 1980s were a time of dramatic events worldwide. Tragedies such as the explosions of the space shuttle *Challenger* and the Chernobyl nuclear power plant shocked the world out of its complacent belief that humankind had mastered nature and firmly controlled its technological creations. In U.S. politics, scandal rocked the White House when several high-ranking officials in the Ronald Reagan administration were convicted of selling arms to Iran and aiding the Nicaraguan Contra rebels. In global politics, U.S. president Ronald Reagan and Soviet president Mikhail Gorbachev signed a landmark treaty banning intermediate-range nuclear forces, marking the beginning of an era of arms control. In several parts of the world—including Beijing, China, the West Bank and Gaza Strip, and several nations of Eastern Europe—people rose up to resist oppressive governments, with varying degrees of success. In American culture, crack cocaine and inner-city poverty contributed to the development of a new and controversial music genre: gangsta rap.

Many of these events were unrelated to one another except for the fact that they occurred at about the same time. Others were linked to global developments. Greenhaven Press's World History by Era series provides students with a unique tool for examining global history in a way that allows them to appreciate the seemingly random occurrences as well as the general trends of human progress. This series divides world history—from the time of ancient Greece and Rome to the end of the second millennium—into ten discrete periods. Each volume then presents a collection of both primary and secondary documents that describe the major events of the period in chronological order. This structure provides students with a snapshot of events occurring simultaneously in all parts of the world. The reader can then see the connections between events in far-flung corners of the world. For example, the Palestinian uprising (*Intifada*) of December 1987 was near in time—if not in character and location—to similar protests in Beijing, China; Berlin, Germany; Prague, Czechoslovakia; and Bucharest, Romania. While these events were different in many ways, they all involved ordinary citizens striving for self-autonomy and democracy against governments that were attempting to impose strict controls on their civil liberties. By making the connections between these events, students can see that they comprised a global movement for democracy and human rights that profoundly impacted social and political systems worldwide.

Each volume in this series offers features to enhance students' understanding of the era of world history under discussion. An introductory essay provides an overview of the period, supplying essential context for the readings that follow. An annotated table of contents highlights the main point of each selection. A more in-depth introduction precedes each document, placing it in its particular historical context and offering biographical information about the author. A thorough chronology and index allow students to quickly reference specific events and dates. Finally, a bibliography opens up additional avenues of research. These features help to make the World History by Era series an extremely valuable tool for students researching the rise and fall of civilizations, social and political revolutions, cultural movements, scientific and technological advancements, and other events that mark the unfolding of human history throughout the world.

INTRODUCTION

Take up the White Man's Burden—
*   Send forth the best ye breed—*
Go bind your sons to exile
*   To serve your captives' need;*
To wait in heavy harness,
*   On fluttered folk and wild—*
Your new-caught, sullen peoples,
*   Half-devil and half-child.*

—Rudyard Kipling, 1899

During the period from 1848, the beginning of sweeping political change, to the start of World War I in 1914, a few western European countries came to dominate almost the entire globe. Virtually all of Asia and Africa were carved up into European colonial empires, while the rest of the world lay in thrall to European economic interests. The United States and Japan shared in this domination to a small degree, but the great global powers of the age were Great Britain, France, Germany, Italy, Belgium, and the Netherlands.

In addition to their territorial and economic domination, European nations, along with the United States, demonstrated an unprecedented creativity in science and technology. Industrialism spread rapidly, and the world grew increasingly connected by European inventions such as the telegraph, the railroad, the steamship, and, by 1914, the telephone, radio, and airplane. Although the emergence of Japan posed a mild threat to European power, and despite the fact that competition among European powers frequently threatened to break out into open war, Europe's domination of the globe appeared to be an accomplished fact in 1914.

European energy and creativity also inspired a high degree of self-confidence. Most Europeans believed that their civilization, characterized as it was by industrialism, free trade, the Christian

15

religion, and political systems based in principle (if not always in practice) on the rights and freedoms of all individuals, truly was superior to the civilizations of China, India, and the rest of the globe. They believed their destiny was to shoulder, as Rudyard Kipling writes above, the "white man's burden," and bring the benefits of their civilization to the world.

THE PAX BRITANNICA

The greatest of the colonial powers was Great Britain. Indeed, the reign of Queen Victoria (1837–1902) has been described as the "Pax Britannica," or "British peace," and the fact that English is today the globe's common language has much to do with Britain's dominance during the period. This small but assertive island nation led the way in science and technology and, in 1848, was the only truly industrialized nation on Earth. Furthermore, the British colonial empire was already expanding by 1848, despite the loss of the thirteen rich colonies that made up the original United States of America. Canada, Australia, New Zealand, and parts of southern Africa made up what the British referred to as their "white dominions." Elsewhere, islands and coastal outposts guaranteed British control of the oceans while a victorious war against China, the Opium War of 1840–1842, gave the British control of Hong Kong.

British control of India, which began with a few East India Company trading posts in the 1600s, expanded slowly but steadily as the Company added piece after piece of the subcontinent to its holdings. After crushing a rebellion in 1857, the British Crown took direct control of most of India. Indeed, India went on to become the centerpiece of the British Empire, the "jewel in the crown," and Queen Victoria officially added the title of Empress of India to her long list of honors in 1872.

Several events mark the growth and apogee of British global power. In 1851 Britain staged the first ever world's fair: London's Crystal Palace Exhibition. The event was intended to both celebrate and demonstrate Britain's predominance in industry and technology as well as its colonial empire. To a fascinated public, thousands of exhibitors showed off devices such as high-powered weaponry, working models of trains and bridges, and consumer items such as rotating toast racks. Over six million visitors from all over the world walked through the Crystal Palace, a vast structure of glass and iron housing the exhibition. It was a resounding success, and it enabled Britain to show the world that, in 1851, it had no rivals in either creativity or practical application.

A second event that celebrated British power was the opening of the Suez Canal in 1869. It might seem strange to describe the canal as a triumph for the British Empire as it cut through Egyptian territory and was the product of a French-Egyptian consortium guided by French promoter Ferdinand de Lesseps. Yet Britain's strategic interests in the canal grew to be the overriding factor in its maintenance; Britain bought out the Egyptian shares in the canal company at its first opportunity and, to ensure that the canal would operate in its interest, took effective control of Egyptian politics in the 1880s. The canal greatly shortened the sea voyage between Britain and its imperial possessions in Asia. Once the canal was opened, ocean liners no longer had to sail completely around the continent of Africa to reach the Indian Ocean. They could instead pass easily from the Mediterranean Sea into the Red Sea. With the simultaneous development of steamships, the Suez Canal shortened the journey to India from at least six months to only a few weeks. The huge steamships of Britain's Peninsular and Oriental Line (P&O) became part of the regular traffic through the canal and contributed a new word to the English language as the best berths on P&O liners were "port out, starboard home," or posh.

The high point of British power was the celebration of Queen Victoria's Diamond Jubilee in 1897. Victoria's sixty years on the throne saw Britain assemble the largest empire the world had ever known, containing approximately one-quarter of the world's land and population. As contemporaries noted, the sun never set on the British Empire. The parades that followed Victoria's carriage through London included dignitaries from across the globe as well as representatives of the British colonies in all their diversity: African tribal chiefs, Chinese soldiers, Inuit from Canada, Maori from New Zealand, and Indian rajas with their own armies.

CHALLENGES TO BRITISH POWER

But British power as demonstrated in 1897 was perhaps hollower than it appeared. The British had nearly been forced out of India in 1857 during an uprising known as the Sepoy Rebellion, or, as the British referred to it, the Sepoy Mutiny. Sepoys were Indian soldiers who formed the bulk of Britain's army in India; enlisting Indians was necessary from the British standpoint because of the difficulties of importing and maintaining an army of Europeans so far from home. Although sepoys were barred from officers' ranks, during the early nineteenth century they were treated with respect: Hindus, for instance, were allowed to cook their own food according to the guidelines of their caste. Yet by 1857 the British had grown less respectful of Indian traditions and more confident of the superiority of their own ways. Christian missionaries, for instance, aggressively sought converts among the sepoys, among whom resentment grew for British disrespect of their traditional cultures. A flashpoint was reached when the British army introduced the new Enfield rifle. Loading it required the gunman to bite the tip off a cartridge that contained the bullet and gunpowder. Sepoys believed that the cartridges were greased with a combination of pig fat, anathema to Muslim soldiers, and cow fat, polluting to Hindus. Now convinced that the British were trying to destroy their religions, many sepoys rose up against their officers and, briefly, took control of large portions of northern India.

British forces were able to reestablish control but were now convinced that Indian rule required a stern and paternal hand. British imperialism in India and elsewhere grew arrogant as British India entered the era of Kipling's "white man's burden." British occupation rested in part on a conviction that Britain's imperial duty was to bring the benefits of Western civilization—industry, technology, science, liberal democracy, and the Christian religion—to the colonized (and presumed backward) Indians. Needless to say, colonized peoples, in India as elsewhere, did not always agree. The Indian independence movement was already underway by the 1880s.

If Britain's colonial authority remained thin under the pageantry of empire, British domination faced increasing challenges from other western European nations. France in particular attempted to build its own colonial empire while Germany, following its 1871 unification, quickly emerged as a major industrial power. Other European nations such as Italy, the Netherlands, Belgium, and Portugal built or maintained colonial empires of their own while Russia and Austria exercised their imperial instincts on the Eurasian landmass. Britain's success, indeed, inspired imitation and competition until tensions finally boiled over with the outbreak of World War I.

France had been Britain's greatest international rival since the 1600s. While it had lost many of its earlier possessions, such as Canada and the Louisiana Territory in North America, it was quick to establish a new international presence in the mid-1800s, particularly with the accession to the throne of the emperor Napoléon III in 1851. The North African nation of Algeria fell in the 1840s to a French coup and came to be considered virtually a province of France itself. Thereafter France considered North Africa to lie within its sphere of interest. As the decades of the nineteenth century passed, France went on to dominate most of northern and western Africa.

On the opposite side of the world, the most important French possession was the colony referred to as French Indochina, consisting of the modern nations of Vietnam, Laos, and Cambodia. There, the French sought to counter the growing British influence in Asia as well as take advantage of the rich natural resources of Vietnam and the Mekong River area. Like their British counterparts, the French undertook what they called a "civilizing mission," by which they tried to establish various institutions of French culture, including Roman Catholicism and a centralized bureaucracy, in Indochina.

While France effectively challenged Britain as a colonizing power, it failed to become a dominant industrial power and found its position relative to Britain and Germany weakened by 1914. Although certain parts of France industrialized early, the new factory economy was slow in coming to Paris, the capital. Moreover, most French people remained rural peasants rather than city-dwelling factory workers until well after World War I.

THE RISE OF GERMANY

Another problem France faced was the reemergence of a major enemy right on its border: the new nation of Germany. Germany was completely unified in 1871, following a successful war with France, and suddenly constituted a military and industrial juggernaut that appeared capable of challenging France for influence on the European continent and Britain for control of the seas. Germany's rise to power was a major factor in spurring competition for colonies. In addition, Germany's aggressive and confrontational foreign policy greatly increased the tensions that helped start World War I.

Germany's unification was a manifestation of the greater nationalist trend of the nineteenth century. During the era most Europeans grew to believe that the centralized nation-state was the best possible form of government for national progress as well as survival as competition among European peoples grew more fierce. Peoples were united, nationalists believed, by factors such as geography, a common language and culture, and a common sense of history.

Faith in liberalism strengthened nationalist sentiment, as liberals claimed that individual rights were best protected and advanced within an organized nation-state. Nineteenth-century liberals believed that all men should be equal under the law and were entitled to a political voice in the form of political parties and the right to vote. They wanted to reduce the privileges of forces they saw as conservative and out of date such as the nobility, the army, and organized churches, and increase the political power of the people. Liberals also supported free trade and saw themselves as forces for modernity. The advance of liberalism was slow, and women were not given the vote in any nation until after World War I, but gradually most Europeans saw the liberal nation-state as a superior form of political organization.

European history after 1850 is marked by two great liberal-national unifications. The first was the unification of Italy. In 1848 the Italian peninsula was divided among numerous minor kingdoms, independent city-states, and virtual colonies of the Austrian empire. Yet by 1864 all of Italy, aside from the city of Rome itself, was unified. The movement to unite Italy was known as the "risorgimento," a "rebirth" of Italian greatness. Unifiers such as the sophisticated diplomat Camille Cavour and the popular revolutionary leader Giuseppe Garibaldi sought to not only unify their nation but create a truly modern Italy where the people were sovereign. Their task was finally completed in 1871 when the constitutional (and very limited) monarch Victor Emmanuel ascended the throne in Rome, the pope having finally aquiesced to the emergence of this new state.

Germany's unification was accomplished more violently. The eastern German state of Prussia, long an important military power, led the way, often in opposition to more liberal voices from other parts of the German-speaking world. The prime mover behind German unification was Prussia's "Iron Chancellor," Otto von Bismarck, who handled the day-to-day affairs of Prussia in the name of its emperor, Wilhelm I. Bismarck followed a policy he called "blood and iron" to unify Germany as well as transform it into a major military and industrial power. Using both belligerency and diplomatic machinations, he instigated Prussian wars against Denmark in 1864, the Austrian empire in 1866, and France in 1870. Victory in each war inspired other German states to join Prussia in a new federation. At a ceremony outside Paris in 1871 following a surprising, rapid victory over the French, Wilhelm I was declared the emperor, or kaiser, of a united Germany.

Wilhelm's grandson and successor, who took the name Wilhelm II upon his accession to the throne in 1888, disliked Bismarck and removed him from office. Nonetheless, he took advantage of Bismarck's accomplishments and solidified Germany's status as the world's newest military, industrial, and colonial power. No less than Bismarck, Kaiser Wilhelm II believed that it was Germany's destiny to claim, as he put it, its "place in the sun" along with other global powers, particularly Great Britain.

EUROPEAN COLONIAL POWERS DIVIDE AFRICA

Germany could not hope to compete with Britain, however, in one important area: imperialism. By the time Germany unified and began to seek colonies, much of the world beyond Europe had already been divided up by the other European powers. Blocked in Asia beyond taking control of a few Pacific Ocean islands, Germany sought a greater presence in the one part of the world that still lay largely unexploited by Europeans: the continent of Africa. Germany proved to be a major participant in the so-called scramble for Africa between 1870 and 1900, when the colonial powers raced to colonize the one part of the world still, they believed, theirs for the taking.

In 1848 the European presence in Africa was limited to French Algeria in the north, a couple of small enclaves of resettled slaves in West Africa that were administered by Britain and the United States, a few centuries-old Portuguese trading posts, and the vast lands of southern Africa. Southern Africa, a temperate region rich in farmland and natural resources as well as an important strategic location, was divided among the British and colonies of mostly Dutch settlers known as Boers.

Further European interest in Africa was mostly limited to explorers and missionaries until King Leopold II of Belgium established the Congo Free State in the 1870s, seeking to enrich his home country with the regions' natural resources. Leopold sent soldiers who enslaved, maimed, tortured, and killed hundreds of local people if they did not come up with the daily rubber quotas for him. At the same time, Britain expanded its control of Egypt to ensure access to the Suez Canal. Both actions alarmed the leaders of rival European nations, and soon the scramble for Africa was on. France pushed south from Algeria, Italy acquired strategic colonies across the Mediterranean in Libya and in East Africa, and Germany sought territories rich in natural resources throughout the continent.

What the scramble for Africa made clear was that by the 1870s and 1880s, European nations believed that a colonial empire was necessary to successfully compete for power within Europe. Bismarck, who was dubious about the practical necessity of colonies, finally decided that they were strategically necessary to protect Germany. He declared that "my map of Africa is in Europe," meaning that he believed Germany would be weakened in its struggles against France, Britain, and Russia if it failed to join them in the race to divide Africa. Bismarck was concerned, however, that the disorder of the scramble for Africa might lead to European war. Accordingly, he convened a conference of fourteen nations, including the United States, in Berlin in 1884–1885 to lay ground rules for the division of the continent. Negotiators agreed that a signatory could establish a colony only after notifying other powers and only in previously unclaimed territory.

Delegates also vowed to suppress the African slave trade, bow-
ing to a rising international antislavery movement.

No African kings or tribal chieftains were invited to the Berlin
conference. Their concerns were simply considered irrelevant.
Meanwhile, European colonizers armed with machine guns and
cannons found little difficulty in conquering less well-equipped
African armies. By 1900 only two African countries remained independent: Liberia, a colony founded by former slaves from the
United States, and the ancient Christian kingdom of Ethiopia.

One of the greatest colonial struggles in Africa was the conflict
in the south between the British and Boer settlers. Until the 1890s
the two had gotten along reasonably well, with British settlement
concentrated along the coastline and the Boers established as inland farmers. In the 1890s, however, staunch British imperialist
Cecil Rhodes urged Britain to take control of the entire region.
Mine operator Rhodes had made a fortune in South African dia-
monds and gold, and he wanted to extend his control of the industry. In addition, Rhodes wanted Britain to establish an African
empire that stretched "from the Cape to Cairo," or from Egypt in
the north to the Cape of Good Hope at Africa's southern tip.

Failing to convince the Boers that they should accept British
control, Rhodes instigated the Anglo-Boer War of 1899–1902. The
Boers fought very effectively, and their successes against the
vastly superior forces of the British Empire were a sign to many
that British power was, indeed, hollow. Although Britain finally
won and established the dominion of South Africa, its victory required a huge investment of manpower and money and included
a new phenomenon of war: concentration camps. To prevent the
Boers from fighting a guerrilla war, captured soldiers as well as
women and children were rounded up and interned behind
fences guarded by armed colonial soldiers. When the world
learned of the camps, thanks to an international corps of journalists, the British Empire appeared to lose a little of the moral
authority it so strongly relied on.

THE DECLINE OF CHINA

European imperialism, in Africa and elsewhere, often took advantage of weakness in civilizations that had enjoyed centuries-
long periods of dominance. India was one example, but the
greatest late-nineteenth-century subjugation was that of China.
In the 1700s, Ching dynasty China was perhaps the wealthiest
and certainly the most populous civilization on Earth. Yet by
1900 China was completely dominated by foreign powers, although the Ching emperors still clung to the throne, and by 1914
the Ching dynasty had been overthrown, foreign powers still

dominated, and China's future appeared very unclear.

Signs of weakness in the Ching dynasty began to appear with its defeat by Great Britain in the Opium War of 1840–1842. China's loss demonstrated that it had failed to keep up with European technology, as Britain entered battle with the best ships and weaponry on earth. The defeat opened China widely to foreign trade, and the Ching leaders were forced to accept a series of humiliating treaties with the Western powers. Many Chinese people began to lose their faith in the Ching emperors, whom, it was bitterly remembered, were foreigners from Manchuria.

Another sign of China's weakness was the Taiping Rebellion of 1848–1864. This lengthy conflict was led by Hong Hsiu-ch'an, a schoolteacher who failed the examinations that would have qualified him to become a high-level official, and who promised better conditions for China's peasants. Taiping rebel leaders sought in many ways to directly address the challenge of the West; some adopted Christianity and promised to bring democracy and industrialism to China. At one point in the 1850s the rebellion claimed followers in the millions and took control of the rich Yangtze River Valley in central China. The rebels were finally defeated by Ching forces, who had to rely on European advisers and weaponry, but the price of the rebellion was high: 20 to 30 million people were killed and agriculture virtually stopped in much of the country.

Ching rulers faced numerous other rebellions throughout the remainder of the century, many in response to the growing presence of Western powers. By 1900 most Chinese ports were in foreign hands, and the Chinese economy was under foreign control. Treaty arrangements, moreover, divided much of China into spheres of influence controlled by Britain, France, Russia, Germany, and Japan.

The growing foreign presence, combined with the belief among Europeans by the late 1800s that European culture was the source of progress, was very offensive to many Chinese people, who maintained confidence in the superiority of their own civilization. The final great rebellion of the Ching era was the Boxer Rebellion of 1899–1900, a direct response to Western "cultural" imperialism in the form of Christian missionary activity. In this case the Ching empress dowager, Cixi, a former concubine who ruled China largely through the force of her personality, backed the rebels.

The Boxers, so called by the Western press because they originated in secret organizations known as the Society of Righteous and Harmonious Fists, were vehemently anti-Western. They attacked both Westerners and those Chinese who had allied themselves with the West, whom they referred to as "rice Christians," claiming they had betrayed China in order to get food. Despite a long siege of the foreign quarter of Beijing, however, the rebellion was defeated, in a true sign of the times, by a combined force of troops from Britain, France, Russia, Germany, Japan, and the United States. Cixi was forced to pay reparations and accept the presence of foreign garrisons on Chinese soil. Many local people grew convinced that the Ching dynasty was bankrupt, because Cixi's backing of the Boxers simply increased the Western presence in China rather than removing it.

THE AMERICAN NAVY FORCES OPEN JAPAN

While China failed to respond effectively to Western imperialism, neighboring Japan found ways to counter Western influence. In fact, Japan became the only non-Western nation able to compete with the West on its own terms: By the late nineteenth century Japan was a major industrial, military, and imperial power. The rise of Japan was also a sign to colonized countries such as India and Vietnam that it was not the destiny of Europe to control the globe after all.

In 1848 Japan was ruled by the Tokugawa shoguns, who had taken control in 1600. Opposed to Western influence, the Tokugawa leaders had largely closed off Japan to outsiders and forbidden Japanese people to travel to the West. The one exception was a fleet of Dutch ships that was allowed, once a year, to come to the port of Nagasaki. A small amount of trade took place, but the Japanese were more interested in keeping up with Western developments in science, technology, and politics, which they called "Dutch learning." In other ways, too, such as the accumulation of investment capital and the growth of an urban labor force, Japan was laying the foundation of a modern industrial state during the Tokugawa period.

Japan's voluntary isolation was tested after China was opened to Westerners following the Opium War. In particular the United States, hoping to exploit the China trade, sought a place to refuel and replenish its ships, and Japan seemed the logical choice. Moreover, it seemed wrong to many Westerners that, in an age of industrialism, liberalism, and free trade, a nation should close its borders to outsiders. Consequently, in 1853 the American naval commander Commodore Matthew Perry was authorized to open diplomatic relations with Japan using threats of force. Perry arrived in the harbor at Edo (Tokyo) in command of huge steam-powered warships the likes of which the Japanese had never seen. With Perry's cannons aimed at the wood-and-paper structures of the city, the Japanese quickly realized the country could no longer remain closed to the outside world. It was soon forced, like China, to accept a series of unequal treaties with the Western powers.

Transformation in Japan, however, came quickly. By 1868, following a brief civil war, the Tokugawa leaders were forced to resign, and a new emperor, who took the name Meiji, assumed power. Supporters of the Meiji emperor included young nobles who believed that Japan could learn, selectively, from the West. Their goals were prosperity and strength obtained on the principle of "western learning, eastern values." The new Japanese leaders sent representatives to Europe and the United States to study technology, military organization, and politics while importing a number of experts from the West to train local people. By the 1890s Japan's military, built on the English model in the case of the navy and the German model in the case of the army, was one of the best organized in the world. In addition, Japan quickly established itself as an industrial power, understanding that a powerful economy was the basis for national strength and stability.

The Japanese were also quick to realize the importance of education for a modern state. The nation was the first to introduce mandatory primary and secondary education for both boys and girls, and by 1900 its university system was one of the best in the world, particularly in scientific and technological fields.

Japan's process of modernization took an important final step in 1889 with the promulgation, after years of agitation, of a constitution that guaranteed representative government and recognized individual rights. The constitution differed from many western counterparts, however, in that a great deal of authority was invested in the executive, the Meiji emperor, whom Japanese elites depicted as the source of Japan's power and the focus of national unity. Nonetheless, and even though the liberalism of the constitution was only skin deep, the Japanese could now celebrate their equality with the Western powers.

By the 1890s Japan was powerful enough to demand that its unequal treaties be rescinded and that it be considered an equal in any diplomatic negotiations. Indeed, Japan was ready to become an imperialist power. The Japanese enjoyed a victory against China in 1895, which gave them access to the natural resources of China's far north while expanding their sphere of influence to include many Pacific Ocean islands. The takeover of the independent kingdom of Hawaii by the United States in the 1890s, in fact, was partly due to fears that Japan would get to Hawaii first.

The rise of Japan to the status of a global power was confirmed by the resounding Japanese victory over Russia in the Russo-

Japanese War of 1904–1905. The cause of the war was conflicting claims in Korea and Manchuria, the region north of China, which both nations hoped to exploit. It began when Japan sank virtually the entire Russian navy in a surprise attack at the Russian Pacific Ocean garrison of Port Arthur. Although both Britain and the United States, in effect, supported the Japanese, the outcome of the war was a surprise to the world. For the first time in many decades, a non-Western power defeated a European one in a major war.

Meanwhile, a second non-European power emerged to challenge Britain, France, and Germany. This was the United States of America, which grew dramatically in many ways in the period from 1848 to 1914. Territorial expansion stretched the nation from the Atlantic Ocean to the Pacific Ocean, while immigration from Europe as well as domestic increase resulted in vast leaps in population. By exploiting some of the richest reserves of raw materials and natural resources on earth as well as a creative, energetic population, the United States became one of the world's major industrial powers and, like its competitors, the possessor of a colonial empire.

THE NEW POWER IN NORTH AMERICA

In 1848 America's population was still mostly centered in East Coast cities. Few settlements had been built west of the Mississippi River, as Americans had only in the precious few years taken possession of much of the region. Early that year, however, an employee of a northern California sawmill owned by John Sutter, a German immigrant and entrepreneur, found gold dust in the residue of the milling process. Soon others, including local military officials, found more. News of the discovery of gold in California spread slowly at first, but by 1849 the California gold rush was under way. Thousands of Americans flocked to California to try their luck in the gold fields. They were joined by people from around the world, including a number of "forty-niners" from China.

San Francisco, Oakland, and Sacramento soon turned into boomtowns to support the gold miners. Although most gold seekers were disappointed and gold mining shifted from an entrepreneurial activity to a big business, settlers soon found that California offered other opportunities in agriculture or shipping. In addition, federal authorities in Washington, D.C., realized quickly that California was ideally placed for the trade with China and Japan that they hoped to exploit. By the end of the 1860s the ports of San Francisco and Oakland were bustling with overseas trade and raucous communities of immigrants and settlers, while a railway line, built largely in the west by Chinese laborers, connected California with the cities of the east.

Geographically at a great remove, California's growth was only temporarily hindered by the American Civil War, which tore apart the eastern portion of the United States. The war was devastating for the nation, as hundreds of thousands were killed by battle and disease and a great deal of territory, particularly in the South, was ruined for farming or any other productive activity.

The origins of the American Civil War lay in the different forms of economy and society that had developed in the North and South. While northern cities such as Boston, New York, and Philadelphia were adjusting to the "modern" economy of industry and trade and enjoying the cheap labor provided by millions of European immigrants, the South remained rural and agrarian. In fact, thanks to Britain's textile industry, which required ever-increasing quantities of raw cotton, southerners were encouraged to both expand agriculture and employ slave labor.

As northern calls to end slavery grew more vociferous in the 1850s, southerners began to feel that their very survival was threatened. Finally unwilling to accept domination by the North, many southern states chose to secede from the Union in early 1861 just as a new antislavery president, Abraham Lincoln, was inaugurated. Lincoln refused to allow the United States to be divided into two separate nations, and on April 12, 1861, the North and South went to war. By the time the war was concluded with a Union victory in 1865, over 600,000 people were killed, slavery was abolished, and President Lincoln was dead, assassinated by a southern sympathizer.

The European powers, many of whom were sympathetic to the South for economic reasons, saw the American Civil War as an opportunity to restore their influence in the Western Hemisphere and prevent the United States from expanding its domination of the region. In 1862 France, with the support of Britain and Spain, launched an invasion of Mexico. The Mexicans were initially able to fight off the French, and Mexico still celebrates its victory over the invaders at the Battle of Puebla on May 5 (Cinco de Mayo), 1862. A stronger invasion force, however, returned and installed a puppet emperor, Maximilian I, on the throne of Mexico, where he remained until he was ousted in 1867.

AMERICA GAINS A FOREIGN EMPIRE

Meanwhile, the United States continued to expand economically and demographically as Europe's adventurous and disenfranchised sought a better life in the younger nation across the Atlantic. As the imperialist tide rose in the last decades of the nineteenth century, many Americans felt that their country should join in the competition for overseas colonies. An early example was the kingdom of Hawaii, which was siezed in a bloodless coup by American business interests in 1893. Shortly thereafter the American government accepted Hawaii as a U.S. territory.

It was the Spanish-American War of 1898 that truly qualified the United States as a colonial power. The war's origins lay largely in disagreements over the independence of Cuba, a Spanish colony since the early 1500s. Many Americans thought that Cuba, which lay only ninety miles away from the Florida Keys, should be part of America's sphere of interest, and they either supported Cuban independence movements or urged the takeover of the island by the U.S. government. A pretext for war presented itself when an American naval vessel, the *Maine*, exploded and sank in the harbor at Havana, Cuba. Although the cause was probably a mechanical malfunction, American newspapers blamed Spanish saboteurs and screamed, "Remember the *Maine!*" in banner headlines, calling on the federal government to declare war on Spain. An inflamed public got their wish, and America soon enjoyed a rapid victory over Spain.

The victory gave important parts of Spain's remaining empire to the United States, including the islands of Guam and Puerto Rico, which remain U.S. territories. Cuba, after a brief interlude, achieved its independence while, on the other side of the world, America took possession of Spain's main Asian possession: the Philippine Islands. Just as in the case of Hawaii, Americans were afraid that the Philippines were too weak to govern themselves and that, if America failed to take control, Japan or one of the European powers would. Thus the United States joined Britain, France, the Netherlands, Russia, and Japan as an Asian colonial power.

Another area in which the United States challenged the European powers was in science and technology, as the period from 1848 to 1914 was one of the most innovative in human history. Fuelled both by industry and the requirements of overseas exploration and colonization, Europeans and Americans developed ideas and invented machines that still influence the world today. London's Crystal Palace Exhibition of 1851 was only the beginning.

DARWIN DEVELOPS HIS THEORY OF NATURAL SELECTION

Among the scientists who were first to take advantage of Britain's control of the oceans was the naturalist Charles Darwin. In the early 1830s, Darwin undertook a voyage around the world on the small ship the HMS *Beagle*. He collected specimens of plants and animals and took note of geological patterns wherever he went, which included such obscure parts of the globe as the Galapagos Islands off the Pacific coast of South America. When he returned to Britain he began work on a theory based on his observations. The book explaining his theory, *On the Origin of Species,* was published in 1859. It was among the first and certainly the best-supported examinations of the theory of evolution, or theory of natural selection as Darwin called it.

According to Darwin, all living species are involved in a struggle for existence. Those best able to survive are those best adapted to the circumstances of their environment. This adaptation often depended on the evolution of new biological characteristics, such as larger wings, a hard covering such as a shell, or in the case of human beings, a larger brain. Geological patterns, moreover, proved that the earth was older than biblical scholars claimed and that biological adaptations happened slowly over thousands of years.

Although Darwin himself never thought that his theories challenged religious beliefs, he did imply that human beings evolved from earlier species by adapting in numerous and minute ways to the challenges of their environment, and he argued that biological evolution operated mechanistically rather than through the agency of a god or creator. The publication of *On the Origin of Species,* as well as a second book, *Descent of Man,* in 1871, caused a sensation, and religious and scientific thinkers have passionately debated his theories ever since.

Other innovators were more practical in their orientation, seeking to solve problems created by modern industry and colonialism. Already by 1848 the railroad, steamship, and telegraph had been invented and served to draw the world closer together. Engineers, inventors, and public relations men accelerated the process in numerous ways and by their own innovations.

A REVOLUTION IN COMMUNICATIONS AND TRANSPORTATION

In 1876, Alexander Graham Bell invented the telephone virtually by accident. Bell, a Scottish immigrant to the United States, devoted his energies to the problem of "long-distance telephony" and was able to solve it by figuring a way to send several telegraph signals along a single line. With the help of a local technician, Thomas Watson, Bell tinkered until he inadvertantly transmitted clear vocal sounds over a cable. Bell gained financial support for improving on the telephone by demonstrating it at America's Centennial Celebrations in 1876, and the popularity and usefulness of the "electric talking machine" spread rapidly. By 1900 over one million miles of telephone lines crossed the United States.

Another American, Thomas Edison, made his mark not only as an inventor but also as an organizer and businessman. His inventions include the stock ticker, the phonograph, the kinetoscope (an early motion picture projector), and perhaps most famously, a long-lasting incandescent lightbulb, which Edison's team perfected in 1879. The success of the lightbulb allowed Edison, who operated from a laboratory in Menlo Park, New Jersey, to put electric power to work. His first power station came on line in New York City in the early 1880s and, before long, powered not only electric lights but also streetcars and factories.

Meanwhile, an Italian engineer, Guglielmo Marconi, set out to solve the problem of long-distance wireless communication. He first demonstrated the ability to transmit sounds via radio waves from Italian rooftops in 1895 but soon moved to London, where he hoped to find greater financial support. There, he developed the ability to transmit and receive radio signals over great distances, including across the Atlantic Ocean, which required compensating for the curvature of the earth. While the "wireless," or radio, did not become a major consumer item until the 1920s, by 1914 radios were being widely used by governments, which quickly recognized the benefits of rapid communication in diplomacy, and by shipping companies, which were always receptive to more effective ship-to-shore communication.

The revolution in communications technology was accompanied by a revolution in transportation. Even as new railroad lines crisscrossed the earth and as ever larger steamships both enhanced international travel and provoked a naval race between Britain and Germany, new modes of transport were being developed. Among the first was the "safety" bicycle, which employed both pneumatic tires and brakes, and which enjoyed a spurt of popularity in the industrialized countries in the 1880s and 1890s. Another was the automobile. The first successful internal combustion engine was built in Germany in 1885, but nearly simultaneous efforts in France, Britain, and the United States resulted in rapid improvements in automobile reliability and safety. The automobile proved immediately popular among those who could afford one, and races were already being held by 1895. Unlike the bicycle, however, the automobile largely remained the plaything of the wealthy until the first decades of the twentieth century.

A final step in this revolution in transport was taken in 1903. While hot-air balloons had been in existence for many years, no inventor had yet succeeded in building a flying machine. In that year, however, the Wright brothers of Ohio successfully flew their prototype airplane a distance, on the third try, of 852 feet in 59 seconds. It was the first successful controlled demonstration of a manned heavier-than-air flying machine. Improvements soon followed, and airplanes were to play an important role in World War I, although it was not until the 1920s that air travel became a consumer commodity.

EINSTEIN AND FREUD REINFORCE A GROWING UNCERTAINTY

The Wright brothers' airplanes and Marconi's wireless helped tie together a world that was vastly different in the first decade of the twentieth century than it had been in 1848. Invention followed invention just as colony followed colony, and the hold on the globe of a few western European nations, as well as Japan and the United States, seemed secure. However, numerous signs after 1900 suggested the future might be more uncertain and insecure than the cheering crowds at Queen Victoria's Diamond Jubilee or the American newspapermen who celebrated the victory over Spain might have believed.

Some of these signs of uncertainty, ironically, emerged out of the scientific world. While Darwin and others had described a relatively straightforward, mechanistic universe, a German physicist, Albert Einstein, suggested that the only constant in the universe was change. Einstein's general theory of relativity, published in 1905, pointed out that one's understanding of time and space was relative to the observer as well as to other factors. While Einstein was celebrated as a genius and became the most famous figure in a revolution in physics that was to result in, among many other things, nuclear power, the universe he described was uncertain and random. To some, Einstein's ideas implied that human beings might not have as much control over their world as the accomplishments of industrialism and imperialism had led them to believe.

Another innovative scientist, the Austrian physician Sigmund Freud, developed the idea that individual behavior was the product of subconscious forces, such as the repressed memory of childhood trauma. Freud published in 1900 a work titled *The Interpretation of Dreams*, one of the earliest works of psychoanalysis. He argued in the book that dreams were in fact statements of the subconscious mind, and that by studying dreams one could gain a better understanding of the suppressed memories that might manifest themselves in mental illness or psychotic behavior. A larger effect of Freud's research, however, was the suggestion that people had less conscious control over themselves and their behavior than they might think. Like that of Einstein, Freud's work was an early example of the theme of uncertainty which characterized so much of the intellectual life of the twentieth century.

WOMEN FIGHT FOR THE RIGHT TO VOTE

The years before 1914 were notable for mounting social problems, among them a widespread struggle for individual political rights in industrialized countries. In addition to labor unions, strikes, and, in Russia in 1905, a failed revolution, the movement for women's suffrage gained momentum. Women in Great Britain were particularly active in demanding the vote. A leader in the movement, Emmeline Pankhurst, started the Women's Social and Political Union in 1903 along with her daughters Christabel and Sylvia. When her campaigns failed to bring results, Pankhurst and her organization turned to militant action in 1910. The suffragettes, as they were labeled by the British press, staged marches and demonstrations, broke windows, and planted explosives. In one instance a woman chained herself to the fence outside the house of Britain's prime minister, demanding that women be given political consideration equal to men. Pankhurst was arrested for her efforts on several occasions and was once force-fed after attempting a prison hunger strike. She and her comrades refused to give in, however, and only the onset of World War I in 1914 ended the militant suffragette movement.

Meanwhile, many critics of European society followed the teachings of Karl Marx, who, along with Friedrich Engels, had predicted as early as 1848 that the contradictions and inequalities of European civilization would result in a workers' revolution and a turn to communism. The English-Irish playwright George Bernard Shaw was one of many figures influenced by Marx. Shaw claimed at the beginning of the twentieth century that, contrary to accepted opinion, European civilization was not characterized by progress. Instead it was as violent, careless, and hypocritical as it had ever been. He only hoped that these conditions could be mitigated by revolution or, failing that, one could take solace in the works of cultural "supermen," the artists.

An actual revolution did break out in Russia in 1905, just as news of losses to Japan reached St. Petersburg and Moscow. Revolutionaries not only protested the hardships of the war, they also spoke out against the autocratic and intolerant rule of Russia's czar, Nicholas II. When a peaceful demonstration turned into a massacre, many of Russia's industrial workers, peasants, and enlisted-level soldiers and sailors rose up in mutiny. Nicholas promised reforms such as a more liberal government, but few of them were carried out. The revolution failed, but some, including Russian Marxists Vladimir Lenin and Leon Trotsky, saw it as a precursor to a larger uprising.

Finally, cracks began to appear in Europe's colonial empires. Again, Britain's victory over the Boers in South Africa had hardly gone as smoothly as was expected, and Japan continued its march through northern Asia and the Pacific. Japan's successes emboldened colonized peoples worldwide, many of whom, particularly in Asia, began to call for the departure of Europeans. In India, for example, the independence movement grew militant when freedom fighters staged demonstrations and riots in 1905 to protest what they perceived as haughty and careless rule on the part of Great Britain.

REVOLUTIONS AND INTERNATIONAL TENSIONS

China's Ching dynasty, meanwhile, finally collapsed when the last emperor, a five-year-old boy named Pu Yi, was overthrown in a revolution in 1911. Modernizers under Sun Yat Sen, a man who had been educated in the West and understood the principles of industry, democracy, and liberalism, tried to turn China into a republic. Sun hoped that by learning from the West, as Japan had, China could survive as a strong nation and control the Western incursions that had sparked the Boxer Rebellion.

A revolution also took place in Mexico when, after a contested election, the long-standing dictator Porfirio Díaz was forced out of office in 1910. While Díaz had attempted to modernize the nation, his programs had largely ignored Mexico's peasants and working and lower-middle classes, who supported the new president, Madero. When Madero was assassinated by conservatives afraid of rapid change, rebellions broke out spontaneously in many parts of the country. For much of the next decade the nation remained in a state of almost constant chaos and uncertainty.

Meanwhile, the competition among the major European powers reached a boiling point. For decades Great Britain, France, Germany, and the other major powers had competed for colonies, for industrial dominance, and for power within Europe. Nationalist sentiment grew ever more terse and intolerant, and many seemed to believe that war, especially between Britain and Germany, was inevitable. It is easy, with hindsight, to trace a few of the steps in this nationalist competition which finally exploded in World War I. Twice, for instance, conflicts over Morocco, a North African nation that hoped to maintain a semblance of autonomy by playing France against Germany, threatened to turn into general war. Moreover, the Ottoman Empire of the Turks was in rapid decline, leaving behind in southeastern Europe peoples intent on asserting their own nationalism: the Serbs, the Bosnians, the Montenegrans, and others. Both Russia and the Austrian Empire sought to fill the void left by the decline of the Ottomans, much to the chagrin of the southeastern Europeans.

And through it all, the newly unified German Empire sought aggressively to assert its "place in the sun," as Kaiser Wilhelm II claimed it should. Not only did Germany support Morocco as well as Austrian claims to the Balkans, it engaged in a rapid naval buildup, constructing a number of large and powerful steam warships. Many British observers believed that this naval buildup could only be explained by Germany's plans to fight a war with Britain. It was a fearful prospect for the British, for whom control of the oceans was a point of national identity and pride as well as the lifeblood of empire.

However, until World War I finally broke out in August 1914, Europeans confidently basked in the accomplishments of a world they controlled. Europeans wondered what could possibly surpass such accomplishments as the steam-powered ocean liner *Titanic*, which was constructed in Belfast in British Northern Ireland and set sail on its maiden voyage from Southampton, England, on April 12, 1912. The *Titanic* was the largest passenger ship ever built at nearly 883 feet long, able to displace 46,000 tons of water. While third-class passengers enjoyed a service in "steerage" that far surpassed earlier ships, first-class passengers could take advantage of a level of luxury comparable to the world's finest hotels. The *Titanic*'s owner, the White Star Steamship line, went so far as to advertise the ship as "unsinkable."

The ship did sink, however, in the early morning hours of April 16. It struck an iceberg in its attempt to cross the Atlantic Ocean in record time. Fifteen hundred of its twenty-two hundred passengers and crew were killed as the ship, a triumph of Western art, technology, organization, and finance, slipped under the surface of the Atlantic and settled on the ocean floor over a mile below. And although the sinking of the *Titanic* was a symbol, a symptom rather than a cause, western Europeans never felt quite so confident again.

An Era of Challenge and Transition

==========| CHAPTER 1 |==========

THOUSANDS RACE TO CALIFORNIA IN SEARCH OF GOLD

DONALD BARR CHIDSEY

Early in 1848 James Marshall, a carpenter hired by a businessman named John Sutter to design and manage his sawmill near Sacramento, California, discovered gold dust in the sediment left behind by the milling process. Soon others found more gold dust, and, in one instance, a nugget worth five thousand dollars. The news of the gold discovery was slow to spread to the rest of the United States, as Donald Barr Chidsey asserts in the following selection. Yet once Americans understood the implications of Marshall's find, they began a panic known ever since as the California gold rush of 1849. In addition to thousands of Americans, many Europeans, South Americans, and Chinese found California's promise of easy riches a magnet impossible to resist.

According to Chidsey, the immediate trigger for the gold rush was an announcement by President James Polk that the reports of gold were true. Soon men from all professions and walks of life made plans to travel to California's gold fields. Most, however, did not set out alone but organized themselves as companies to help pay the costs of the journey and excavation.

Donald Barr Chidsey is the author of many works of history and biography, including *The Birth of the Constitution*, *The War with Mexico*, and *Sir Walter Raleigh*.

The discovery of gold in California was first mentioned in a New York newspaper September 16, 1848, and it was no *more* than mentioned. Subsequent journals, there and elsewhere in the East, had small stories about the rumors, but these were not taken seriously, and in most cases they probably were not believed. For Easterners habitually were leery about tales emanating from the West (by which they meant the Mississippi Valley states: Oregon territory and California were referred to as the *Far* West). The West, so travelers reported, was a land inhabited by lank uncouth persons who spoke in a barbarous drawl, using words like "flummock," "cornucked," "conbobberation," "hornswoggle," "monstracious," "the peedaddles," "ripsniptiously," and "helliferocious," and uttering at the top of their lungs challenges to the whole world, together with fantastic claims about the shouter's marksmanship. Almost anything might come out of the West. There was no reason to get het up.

AMERICANS LEARN OF GOLD IN CALIFORNIA

It was not until December, almost a year after [carpenter James] Marshall had plucked those bright flecks out of the tailrace [a device to wash away water and sediment] at Sutter's sawmill, that the public came to believe. And then, when it did, as had happened in California, it went mad.

The [$5,000] nugget Lieutenant Loeser [a California military official] had spotted from his saddle did as much as any one thing to bring about the Rush. The War Department, for reasons of its own, decided to exhibit this nugget to the public. Scores came to view it, then hundreds, at last thousands. Together with some samples of gold dust Colonel Mason [Loeser's commander] had sent with his report, it assayed at 0.894 fine, a figure that was itself doubt-shaking. The word began to get around.

It was President Polk who, in his message opening the second session of the 30th Congress December 5, 1848, really touched off the explosion. The President was a dour, louring man, the first Dark Horse in American politics, who four years before, when the Whig party was split, had defeated by a hair the widely popular and far abler Henry Clay. Polk was not beloved, but he *was* trusted. He was no spread-eagle orator—no slang-whanger, as they would say in the West—and you could depend upon what he wrote. He was not running for a second term; he did not believe in second terms.

What he told Congress about gold in California (it was only about one twentieth of his whole message) was:

> It was known that mines of the precious metals existed
> to a considerable extent in California at the time of its

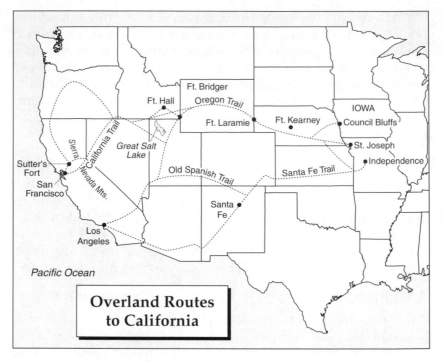

Overland Routes to California

acquisition. Recent discoveries render it probable that these mines are more extensive and valuable than was anticipated. The accounts of the abundance of gold in that territory are of such an extraordinary character as would scarcely command belief were they not corroborated by the authentic reports of officers in the public service, who have visited the mineral district, and derived the facts which they detail from personal observation. Reluctant to credit the reports in general circulation as to the quantity of gold, the officer commanding our forces in California visited the mineral district in July last, for the purpose of obtaining accurate information on the subject. His report to the War Department of the result of his examination, and the facts obtained on the spot, is herewith laid before Congress. When he visited the country there were about four thousand persons engaged in collecting gold. There is every reason to believe that the number of persons so employed has since been augmented. The explorations already made warrant the belief that the supply is very large, and that gold is found at various places in an extensive district of country.

"California" abruptly became a magic word. People who a little earlier couldn't even pronounce it, now babbled pauselessly about the place. At least half of the adult males in the country longed to go there, and many prepared to do so. But they did not dash west immediately. Instead, they organized companies.

MEN FROM ALL WALKS OF LIFE SOUGHT GOLD

A company might number as few as twenty men, as many as two hundred. They were run on democratic but businesslike lines. They elected their own captains and his lieutenants. Many were quasi-military, and a few even had uniforms. Shares were allotted with care, the officers getting no more than the privates, and if a man who wished to go could not afford his share he usually found somebody in town who was willing to stake him—on condition, of course, that he be amply repaid from the gold the company would surely gather as soon as it got to California. Company bands were not uncommon, and here and there a company would get possession of a small cannon, not from fear of Indians but as a signaling device to replace the bugles other companies carried.

These were homogeneous groups, men of roughly the same age, the same walks of life, neighbors who would have common interests, but in the larger companies every effort was made to include carpenters and blacksmiths, especially among those planning to go overland, where wagons would need repairs. Other skills were sometimes sought. For instance, the Boston and California Joint Stock Mining and Trading Company—they usually had long names like that—numbered 150 men, 2 of them clergymen, 4 physicians, 8 ex-whaling captains, and others, such as farmers, shopkeepers, businessmen.

THE DOMINATION OF THE BOURGEOISIE

KARL MARX AND FRIEDRICH ENGELS

In 1848 revolutions calling for greater political rights for the common people swept Europe. In that year two political writers, Karl Marx and Friedrich Engels, together published *The Communist Manifesto*, which was to become one of the most influential writings of all time. Marx and Engels believed that communism, a social system in which workers seized control of factories and governments and thereby regained their self-respect along with the means of production, would arise out of the contradictions and strife of the industrial age. Although the communist idea predated the *Manifesto*, Marx in particular helped turn it into a mainstream ideology that would inspire labor and reform movements worldwide.

In the following selection from *The Communist Manifesto*, Marx and Engels describe how the industrial age was dominated by the social class they refer to as the bourgeoisie: factory owners, bankers, and other "capitalists." They claim that the bourgeoisie has created a new barbarism in which all human relations are reduced to questions of production. Most particularly, it exploits a new class of wage-laborers, the proletarians, who will ultimately revolt against their exploitation.

T he history of all hitherto existing society is the history of class struggles.
Freeman and slave, patrician and plebeian, lord and serf, guild-master and journeyman, in a word, oppressor and oppressed, stood in constant opposition to one another, carried on

Excerpted from *The Communist Manifesto* by Karl Marx and Friedrich Engels, 1848.

an uninterrupted, now hidden, now open fight, a fight that each time ended, either in a revolutionary reconstitution of society at large, or in the common ruin of the contending classes.

In the earlier epochs of history, we find almost everywhere a complicated arrangement of society into various orders, a manifold gradation of social rank. In ancient Rome we have patricians, knights, plebeians, slaves; in the Middle Ages, feudal lords, vassals, guild-masters, journeymen, apprentices, serfs; in almost all of these classes, again, subordinate gradations.

The modern bourgeois society that has sprouted from the ruins of feudal society has not done away with class antagonisms. It has but established new classes, new conditions of oppression, new forms of struggle in place of the old ones.

Our epoch, the epoch of the bourgeoisie, possesses, however, this distinctive feature: it has simplified the class antagonisms. Society as a whole is more and more splitting up into two great hostile camps, into two great classes directly facing each other: Bourgeoisie and Proletariat.

THE RISE OF THE BOURGEOISIE

From the serfs of the Middle Ages sprang the chartered burghers of the earliest towns. From these burgesses the first elements of the bourgeoisie were developed.

The discovery of America, the rounding of the Cape, opened up fresh ground for the rising bourgeoisie. The East-Indian and Chinese markets, the colonization of America, trade with the colonies, the increase in the means of exchange and in commodities generally, gave to commerce, to navigation, to industry, an impulse never before known, and thereby, to the revolutionary element in the tottering feudal society, a rapid development.

The feudal system of industry, under which industrial production was monopolized by closed guilds, now no longer sufficed for the growing wants of the new markets. The manufacturing system took its place. The guild-masters were pushed on one side by the manufacturing middle class; division of labour between the different corporate guilds vanished in the face of division of labour in each single workshop.

Meantime the markets kept ever growing, the demand ever rising. Even manufacture no longer sufficed. Thereupon, steam and machinery revolutionized industrial production. The place of manufacture was taken by the giant, Modern Industry, the place of the industrial middle class, by industrial millionaires, the leaders of whole industrial armies, the modern bourgeois.

Modern industry has established the world market, for which the discovery of America paved the way. This market has given an immense development to commerce, to navigation, to communication by land. This development has, in its turn, reacted on the extension of industry; and in proportion as industry, commerce, navigation, railways extended, in the same proportion the bourgeoisie developed, increased its capital, and pushed into the background every class handed down from the Middle Ages.

We see, therefore, how the modern bourgeoisie is itself the product of a long course of development, of a series of revolutions in the modes of production and of exchange.

Each step in the development of the bourgeoisie was accompanied by a corresponding political advance of that class. An oppressed class under the sway of the feudal nobility, an armed and self-governing association in the medieval commune; here independent urban republic (as in Italy and Germany), there taxable 'third estate' of the monarchy (as in France), afterwards, in the period of manufacture proper, serving either the semi-feudal or the absolute monarchy as a counterpoise against the nobility, and, in fact, corner-stone of the great monarchies in general, the bourgeoisie has at last, since the establishment of Modern Industry and of the world market, conquered for itself, in the modern representative State, exclusive political sway. The executive of the modern State is but a committee for managing the common affairs of the whole bourgeoisie.

The bourgeoisie, historically, has played a most revolutionary part.

The bourgeoisie, wherever it has got the upper hand, has put an end to all feudal, patriarchal, idyllic relations. It has pitilessly torn asunder the motley feudal ties that bound man to his 'natural superiors', and has left remaining no other nexus between man and man than naked self-interest, than callous 'cash payment'. It has drowned the most heavenly ecstasies of religious fervour, of chivalrous enthusiasm, of philistine sentimentalism, in the icy water of egotistical calculation. It has resolved personal worth into exchange value, and in place of the numberless indefeasible chartered freedoms, has set up that single, unconscionable freedom—Free Trade. In one word, for exploitation, veiled by religious and political illusions, it has substituted naked, shameless, direct, brutal exploitation.

THE BOURGEOISIE REDUCES EVERYTHING TO FINANCIAL RELATION

The bourgeoisie has stripped of its halo every occupation hitherto honoured and looked up to with reverent awe. It has converted the physician, the lawyer, the priest, the poet, the man of science, into its paid wage-labourers.

The bourgeoisie has torn away from the family its sentimental veil, and has reduced the family relation to a mere money relation.

The bourgeoisie has disclosed how it came to pass that the brutal display of vigour in the Middle Ages, which Reactionists so much admire, found its fitting complement in the most slothful indolence. It has been the first to show what man's activity can bring about. It has accomplished wonders far surpassing Egyptian pyramids, Roman aqueducts, and Gothic cathedrals; it has conducted expeditions that put in the shade all former Exoduses of nations and crusades.

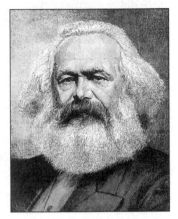

Karl Marx

The bourgeoisie cannot exist without constantly revolutionizing the instruments of production, and thereby the relations of production, and with them the whole relations of society. Conservation of the old modes of production in unaltered form, was, on the contrary, the first condition of existence for all earlier industrial classes. Constant revolutionizing of production, uninterrupted disturbance of all social conditions, everlasting uncertainty and agitation distinguish the bourgeois epoch from all earlier ones. All fixed, fast-frozen relations, with their train of ancient and venerable prejudices and opinions are swept away, all new-formed ones become antiquated before they can ossify. All that is solid melts into air, all that is holy is profaned, and man is at last compelled to face with sober senses, his real conditions of life, and his relations with his kind.

The need of a constantly expanding market for its products chases the bourgeoisie over the whole surface of the globe. It must nestle everywhere, settle everywhere, establish connexions everywhere.

The bourgeoisie has through its exploitation of the world market given a cosmopolitan character to production and consumption in every country. To the great chagrin of Reactionists, it has drawn from under the feet of industry the national ground on which it stood. All old-established national industries have been destroyed or are daily being destroyed. They are dislodged by new industries, whose introduction becomes a life and death question for all civilized nations, by industries that no longer work up indigenous raw material, but raw material drawn from the remotest zones; industries whose products are consumed, not only at home, but in every quarter of the globe. In place of the old wants, satisfied by the productions of the country, we find new wants, requiring for their satisfaction the products of distant lands and climes. In place of the old local and national seclusion and self-sufficiency, we have intercourse in every direction, universal inter-dependence of nations. And as in material, so also in intellectual production. The intellectual creations of individual nations become common property. National one-sidedness and narrow-mindedness become more and more impossible, and from the numerous national and local literatures, there arises a world literature.

The bourgeoisie, by the rapid improvement of all instruments of production, by the immensely facilitated means of communication, draws all, even the most barbarian, nations into civilization. The cheap prices of its commodities are the heavy artillery with which it batters down all Chinese walls, with which it forces the barbarians' intensely obstinate hatred of foreigners to capitulate. It compels all nations, on pain of extinction, to adopt the bourgeois mode of production; it compels them to introduce what it calls civilization into their midst, i.e., to become bourgeois themselves. In one word, it creates a world after its own image.

The bourgeoisie has subjected the country to the rule of the towns. It has created enormous cities, has greatly increased the urban population as compared with the rural, and has thus rescued a considerable part of the population from the idiocy of rural life. Just as it has made the country dependent on the towns, so it has made barbarian and semi-barbarian countries dependent on the civilized ones, nations of peasants on nations of bourgeois, the East on the West.

The bourgeoisie keeps more and more doing away with the scattered state of the population, of the means of production, and of property. It has agglomerated population, centralized means of production, and has concentrated property in a few hands. The necessary consequence of this loosely was political centralization. Independent, or but loosely connected, provinces with separate interests, laws, governments and systems of taxation, became lumped together into one nation, with one government, one code of laws, one national class-interest, one frontier and one customs-tariff.

The bourgeoisie, during its rule of scarce one hundred years, has created more massive and more colossal productive forces than have all preceding generations together. Subjection of Nature's forces to man, machinery, application of chemistry to industry and agriculture, steam-navigation, railways, electric telegraphs, clearing of whole continents for cultivation, canalization of rivers, whole populations conjured out of the ground—

what earlier century had even a presentiment that such productive forces slumbered in the lap of social labour?

BOURGEOIS SOCIETY CREATES IMPOSSIBLE CONTRADICTIONS

We see then: the means of production and of exchange, on whose foundation the bourgeoisie built itself up, were generated in feudal society. At a certain stage in the development of these means of production and of exchange, the conditions under which feudal society produced and exchanged, the feudal organization of agriculture and manufacturing industry, in one word, the feudal relations of property became no longer compatible with the already developed productive forces; they became so many fetters. They had to be burst asunder; they were burst asunder.

Into their place stepped free competition, accompanied by a social and political constitution adapted to it, and by the economical and political sway of the bourgeois class.

A similar movement is going on before our own eyes. Modern bourgeois society with its relations of production, of exchange and of property, a society that has conjured up such gigantic means of production and of exchange, is like the sorcerer, who is no longer able to control the powers of the nether world whom he has called up by his spells. For many a decade past the history of industry and commerce is but the history of the revolt of modern productive forces against modern conditions of production, against the property relations that are the conditions for the existence of the bourgeoisie and of its rule. It is enough to mention the commercial crises that by their periodical return put on its trial, each time more threateningly, the existence of the entire bourgeois society. In these crises a great part not only of the existing products, but also of the previously created productive forces, are periodically destroyed. In these crises there breaks out an epidemic that, in earlier epochs, would have seemed an absurdity—the epidemic of overproduction. Society suddenly finds itself put back into a state of momentary barbarism; it appears as if a famine, a universal war of devastation had cut off the supply of every means of subsistence; industry and commerce seem to be destroyed; and why? Because there is too much civilization, too much means of subsistence, too much industry, too much commerce. The productive forces at the disposal of society no longer tend to further the development of the conditions of bourgeois property; on the contrary, they have become too powerful for these conditions, by which they are fettered, and so soon as they overcome these fetters, they bring disorder into the whole of bourgeois society, endanger the existence of bourgeois prop-

erty. The conditions of bourgeois society are too narrow to com-
prise the wealth created by them. And how does the bourgeoisie
get over these crises? On the one hand by enforced destruction
of a mass of productive forces; on the other, by the conquest of
new markets, and by the more thorough exploitation of the old
ones. That is to say, by paving the way for more extensive and
more destructive crises, and by diminishing the means whereby
crises are prevented.

The weapons with which the bourgeoisie felled feudalism to
the ground are now turned against the bourgeoisie itself.

But not only has the bourgeoisie forged the weapons that
bring death to itself; it has also called into existence the men
who are to wield those weapons—the modern working class—
the proletarians.

In proportion as the bourgeoisie, i.e., capital, is developed, in
the same proportion is the proletariat, the modern working class,
developed—a class of labourers, who live only so long as they
find work, and who find work only so long as their labour increases capital. These labourers, who must sell themselves piecemeal, are a commodity, like every other article of commerce, and
are consequently exposed to all the vicissitudes of competition,
to all the fluctuations of the market.

Industry and Empire on Display: Britain's Crystal Palace Exhibition

Asa Briggs

In 1851 Great Britain was the world's most powerful nation. Its empire spanned the globe and was still growing rapidly. Its ships dominated all of the world's oceans. In addition, Britain was the first country to experience the industrial revolution, and British wealth as well as its scientific and technological achievements surpassed those of any other nation.

Both to celebrate the country's achievements and to demonstrate them to the world, British leaders planned a great exhibition, the first world's fair, for 1851. The exhibition was held in a huge glass and iron structure, the Crystal Palace, which was erected in London's Hyde Park. In the following selection, Asa Briggs describes how the Crystal Palace Exhibition marked an important transition in history from an agrarian and craft-based world to economies organized around industry and commerce. Briggs also notes that the exhibition offered the British the chance to expose the world to the great advances, as the British saw them, of their civilization.

Asa Briggs was professor of British history at Oxford University.

Excerpted from *Victorian People: A Reassessment of Persons and Themes, 1851–1867,* by Asa Briggs (New York: Harper & Row). Copyright © 1955 by the University of Chicago. Reprinted with permission from the University of Chicago Press.

The Crystal Palace was a symbol of the age. It suggested at the same time both fairy tale and success story. Behind the glitter there was human thought and human work. From the first flash of the bright idea it took [designer Joseph] Paxton just over a month to draw up the blueprints, from June 11 to July 15, 1850. The achievement of the contractors was equally remarkable. The ground was handed over to them on July 30; the first column was raised on September 26. Within seventeen weeks of the start, nearly a million feet of glass had been fastened on to the weblike structure of thirty-three hundred columns and twenty-three hundred girders. The secret of the speed of construction was prefabrication. All material used on the Palace was interchangeable: the girders, columns, gutters, and sash bars were identical throughout the whole building. Even before the Palace was completed, the exhibits themselves started to pour in, and on May 1, the official day of opening, the only exhibits which had not arrived were those from Russia. The planning had been perfect.

There were over thirteen thousand exhibitors, one half of the total Exhibition area being occupied by Great Britain and the colonies, and the other half by foreign states, of which France and Germany were the most important. The exhibits were classified according to a scheme of the young scientist Lyon Playfair, one of the rising men of 1851, an industrious professor who was also an outstanding public servant. Rejecting elaborate systems of

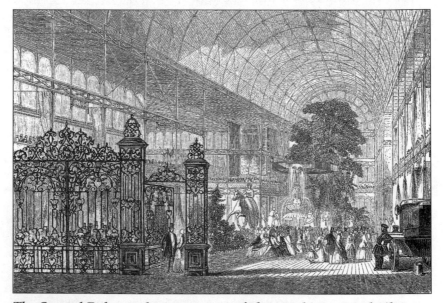

The Crystal Palace, a huge structure of glass and iron, was built to exhibit the most innovative products of science, commerce, and the arts for the first world's fair in 1851.

classification based upon Continental abstraction, he divided the objects on show into four groups—raw materials, machinery, manufactures, and fine arts.

Taken as a whole, the objects suggested the meeting of old and new. Machinery was in the ascendant, but handicrafts were not yet in general eclipse. Alongside a sewing machine from the United States and cotton machines from Oldham there was fine black lace from Barcelona and pottery from Sèvres. . . .

THE APPEAL OF TECHNOLOGY

The Machinery Court was the noisiest and most popular spectacle inside the Crystal Palace. Crowds of farmers in smocks could be seen admiring the agricultural implements, which included a pioneer reaping machine from the United States; mechanics from Leeds and Birmingham gathered round the Jacquard loom and De la Rue's envelope machine; the Queen herself was specially interested in a medal-making machine, which produced fifty million medals a week. She marveled, too, at the electric telegraph and sent appropriate messages to her loyal subjects in Edinburgh and Manchester. Many of the machines displayed were more clever than useful. For example, among the gadgets on view were "an alarm bedstead, causing a person to arise at any given hour," and a "cricket catapulta, for propelling the ball in the absence of a first-rate bowler.". . .

Candles and gaslight and dreams of electricity; medieval armor and Birmingham hardware; pyramids of soap and massive ecclesiastical ornaments, which made the commissioners afraid of cries of "No Popery"—all these were part of 1851. And many recent writers who have made it fashionable to admire Victorian Gothic have considered that the medieval preoccupations of the men of 1851 were at least as fruitful as their confident expectations of continued material progress. It is difficult to judge. Of two young men who visited the Exhibition, one, William Whiteley, aged twenty, was so inspired by the glass building that he began to dream of large retail stores, "universal providers' shops," with plate-glass fronts. The other, William Morris, three years younger, was moved sufficiently by the Exhibition to call the whole display "wonderfully ugly." His revolt not only against mid-Victorian design but against mid-Victorian society demonstrated the sharp change of mood in the later nineteenth century.

Both old and new, revival and anticipation, had to be adequately represented if the Exhibition were to fulfil the objectives laid down by its great architect, the Prince Consort [Albert, Queen Victoria's husband], and his indefatigable colleague, Henry Cole, who has been properly described as "a Prince Consort on a lowlier plane." Their ambitious project of an international exhibition developed out of very humble origins. The Royal Society of Arts, which had exhibited its prize awards for agricultural and industrial machinery since 1761, held two special tiny exhibitions in 1844 and 1845; it was interested in the possibility of "wedding high art with mechanical skill." Cole, a civil servant with a taste for administrative centralization, submitted a model of a tea set and not only won the silver medal but became a leading member of the society. He infused an energy into the society's projects which justified the use of the motto on the title-page of his biography: "Whatsoever thy hand findeth to do, do it with thy might." He and the Prince Consort, working first through the Royal Society and then through a royal commission, were directly responsible for the scale and magnificence of the final Exhibition. "For the *first* time in the world's history," Cole told the members of the Society of Arts, "the men of Arts, Science and Commerce were permitted by their respective governments to meet together to discuss and promote those objects for which civilized nations exist."

THE FAILED TAIPING REBELLION IN CHINA

JOHN KING FAIRBANK

In the 1800s China's rulers, the Ching, or Manchu, dynasty, suffered a number of blows that threatened both their reign and the stability of China in general. Among the first was Great Britain's victory over China in the Opium War of 1839–1842, which opened China to Western trade and cultural influence. Christian missionaries followed European and American merchants and attracted many converts. One such convert, a failed bureaucrat named Hung Hsiu-ch'uan, started a rebellion in 1848, the Taiping Rebellion, which soon involved millions of Chinese and took control of the rich valley of the Yangtze River in the center of the country. To quell the rebellion, which lasted until 1864 and cost hundreds of thousands of lives, Ching leaders were forced to seek Western military assistance.

According to the following selection, written by preeminent historian of China John King Fairbank, the Taiping Rebellion failed to change China's national life. The leaders of the rebellion, using an odd combination of Christian and Chinese ideas, neglected to seek the support of important elements of Chinese society, such as the scholar-gentry, and made a number of strategic errors, such as failing to take control of the important port city of Shanghai.

John King Fairbank is the author of dozens of books on Chinese history.

T he Taiping founder was Hung Hsiu-ch'uan, the faith he preached was his own version of Old Testament Protestant Christianity, and his Heavenly Kingdom of Great Peace

Excerpted from *The Great Chinese Revolution*, by John King Fairbank. Copyright © 1986 by John King Fairbank. Reprinted by permission of HarperCollins Publishers, Inc.

ruled at Nanking from 1853 to 1864. But many things doomed it from the start, as though Chinese society were prepared to give birth to a new dynasty but the foreign environment of the nineteenth century instead produced an abortion. The chance for a new national life was missed.

After Hung had failed a fourth time in the Canton examinations in 1843, he exploded in rage at the Manchu domination of China and then read some Christian missionary tracts, which seemed to explain the visions he had had during an earlier mental illness: God the Father had evidently called him to save mankind and Jesus was his Elder Brother. Hung became a militant evangelist for a moral life to serve the one true God. A month with a Baptist missionary with the memorable name of Issachar Jacox Roberts in 1847 gave him examples of how to pray, preach, sing hymns, catechize, confess one's sins, baptize, and otherwise practice fundamentalist Protestantism. The tracts, which remained Hung's major source of Christian doctrine, had been written by the early Cantonese convert Liang Fa, who saw in the Old Testament a story of a chosen few who with God's help had rebelled against oppression. Liang stressed the righteous wrath of Jehovah, more than the loving-kindness of Jesus, and gave Hung barely a fingerhold on Christian theology. But with his first two converts Hung created an iconoclastic monotheism potent enough to set up the Taiping theocracy yet too blasphemous to win foreign support, too intent on the one true God to permit cooperation with secret societies like the Triads, and too bizarre and irrational to win over Chinese literati, who were normally essential to setting up a new administration.

The God-Worshipers' Society, as the sect first called itself, got started in a mountain region of Kwangsi, west of Canton, variously populated by Yao and Chuang aborigines and Chinese Hakkas like the Hung family, that is, migrants from North China several centuries before, who retained a northern dialect and other ethnic traits like opposition to footbinding. As a minority in South China, the scattered Hakka communities were uncommonly sturdy and enterprising, as well as prone to defend themselves.

How Hung became the rebel king of half China is a story like that of Napoleon Bonaparte or Adolf Hitler, full of romantic drama, the mysteries of chance, and personal and social factors much debated ever since. His converts had the faith that God had ordered them to destroy Manchu rule and set up a new order of brotherhood and sisterhood among God's children. Leadership was taken by six activists who became sworn brothers, among whom Hung was only the first among equals. The chief military leader was an illiterate charcoal burner named Yang, who had the wit to receive God's visitations and speak with His voice in a way that left Hung sincerely speechless. Several of the other leaders were low-level scholars. None was a mere peasant. They got their political-military system from the ancient classic *The Rituals of Chou*. Their movement was highly motivated, highly organized, and austerely puritanical, at first even segregating men from women.

A STRANGE COMBINATION OF IDEAS AND PRACTICES

Taiping Christianity half-borrowed and half-recreated for Chinese purposes a full repertoire of prayers, hymns, and rituals, and preached the brotherhood and sisterhood of all mankind under the fatherhood of the one true and only God. Unlike the passivity of Taoism or the otherworldliness of Buddhism, the Protestant Old Testament offered trumpet calls to a militant people on the march against their oppressors. The original corps of Hakka true believers from Kwangsi were the bravest in battle and the most considerate toward the common people. And no wonder! Hung's teaching created a new Chinese sect organized for war. It used tried and true techniques evolved during 1,800 years of Christian history to inculcate an ardent faith in each individual and ensure his/her performance in its service. Taiping Christianity was a unique East-West amalgam of ideas and practices geared to militant action, the like of which was not seen again until China borrowed and Sinified Marxism-Leninism a century later.

Hung probably never said, "A single spark can start a prairie fire," but [twentieth-century Chinese Communist dictator] Mao Tse-tung could have got the idea from the God-Worshipers' success story. Kwangsi in 1850 was far from Peking, lightly garrisoned by Manchu troops, and strongly affected by the influx of opium runners and pirates driven inland along the West River by the British navy's pirate hunting along the coast. The growing disorder inspired the training of local self-defense forces, including both militia and bandits, with little to choose between them since all lived off the people. The small congregation of God-Worshipers, like other groups, armed for self-defense, but secretly and for a larger purpose. By late 1850 some twenty thousand true believers answered Hung's call to mobilize, and they battled imperial troops sent to disperse them. On January 11, 1851, his thirty-eighth birthday, Hung proclaimed himself Heavenly King of a new dynasty, the Heavenly Kingdom of Great Peace.

The militant Taiping faith inspired an army of fierce warriors who in the early years kept to a strict moral discipline, befriended the common people, and by their dedication attracted recruits and terrified opponents. They carried a multitude of flags and banners, partly for identification of units. Instead of wearing the queue that the Manchu dynasty required as a badge of loyalty (such a tangible symbol!), the Taipings let their hair grow and became the "longhaired rebels," even more startling for establishmentarians to behold than student rebels of the Western counterculture a century or so later.

THE COST OF THE REBELLION

In China the fifteen-year civil war from 1850 to 1864 was tremendously destructive to life and property. Some six hundred walled cities changed hands, often with massacres. While the American Civil War of the early 1860s was the first big contest of the industrial era, when rail and steamship transport and precision-made arms were key factors, the Taiping-imperialist war in China was the last of the pre-modern kind. Armies moved on their feet and lived off the land. No medical corps attended them. Modern maps and the telegraph were lacking. Artillery was sometimes used in sieges but the favorite tactic was to tunnel under a wall, plant gunpowder, and blow it up. Navies of junks and sampans fought on the Yangtze and its major lakes to the south, but steamships were a rarity. Muskets were used but much of the carnage was in hand-to-hand combat with swords, knives, pikes, and staves. This required motivation more than technical training. An invading army might make up its losses by local recruitment, conscription, or conversion of captives, but a commander could not always count on such troops' standing their ground, much less charging the enemy. Imperial generals brought in Manchu and Mongol hereditary warriors, but the humid South often undid them and their cavalry was no good in rice fields. The struggle was mainly Chinese against Chinese. Official reports of armies of 20,000 and 30,000 men, sometimes 200,000 and 300,000, make one wonder how they were actually fed and what routes they traveled by, in a land generally without roads. Troop totals were always in round numbers and should probably be scaled down.

In 1851 the Taiping horde erupted northward, captured the Wuhan cities, and early in 1853 descended the Yangtze to take Nanking and make it their Heavenly Capital. Their strategy was what one might expect of an ambitious committee dominated by an illiterate charcoal burner: ignorant of the outer world, they left Shanghai [an important port] in imperial hands and failed to develop any foreign relations. Dizzy with success, they sent inadequate forces simultaneously north to conquer Peking and west to recover Central China. Both expeditions failed. Commanders operated pretty much on their own, without reliable intelligence, communications, or coordination, simply coping with situations that arose. Absorbed in religion and warfare, the Taiping leaders were inept in economics, politics, and overall planning.

Lacking trained administrators, they generally failed to take over and govern the countryside as a base area for supplies of men and food. Instead they campaigned from city to city, living off the proceeds of loot and requisitions, much like the imperial armies. All this resulted from their narrow religiosity, which antagonized, instead of recruiting, the Chinese scholar-gentry class who could have run a government for them. One result was that the local landed elite remained in place in the countryside. No social revolution occurred. Meanwhile a watering down of their original faith and austerity hit the movement.

Within Nanking the leaders soon each had his own army, palace, harem, and supporters. They spent much time elaborating systems of nobility, honors, and ceremonies. Missionaries who called upon the Taiping prime minister in 1860 found him wearing a gold-embroidered crown and clad like his officers in robes of red and yellow silk. Egalitarianism had continued for the rank and file only.

The original leadership had destroyed itself in 1856 when the Eastern King, Yang, the chief executive and generalissimo, plotted to usurp the position of the Heavenly King, Hung, who therefore got the Northern King, Wei, to assassinate Yang and his supporters, only to find that Wei and his supporters, drunk with power, had to be assassinated by the Assistant King, Shih, who then felt so threatened that he took off to the west with much of the army, leaving Hung sitting on a rump of his own incompetent kinfolk. . . .

The Taiping Heavenly Kingdom went the way of Carthage— only the name survived. The record is biased because the imperialists destroyed all Taiping writings, except for those preserved mainly by foreigners (some were found only in this century in French and British libraries). Leaders of ability emerged in the final years, but too late. A cause for which so many gave their lives must have had much to offer, but only in comparison with the effete old order under the Manchus.

JAPAN IS OPENED TO THE WEST

RICHARD STORRY

Since their rise to power in 1600, seeking to prevent social and political instability, the Tokugawa shoguns drastically limited Japan's contact with Western nations. Only one small fleet of Dutch ships was allowed to land every year. Any other European or North American faced imprisonment and deportation if he turned up on Japanese shores. By the mid–1800s, however, neighboring China had been opened to extensive foreign trade, and the invention of the steamship made possible a vast expansion in oceangoing travel. Western powers no longer approved of the isolation of Tokugawa Japan.

In the following selection Richard Storry describes how American naval officers, with the full knowledge and approval of the U.S. government, forced the Tokugawa leaders to end their isolation in 1853. As Storry indicates, Commodore Matthew Perry sought to defeat the representatives of other nations, particularly Russia, to Japan, while American businessmen saw great advantages in access to Japanese markets. Japanese officials finally admitted they were unable to counter Perry's steamships and cannons and gave in to American demands.

Richard Storry was professor of Japanese history at Oxford University.

I t looked as though either Russia or Great Britain would be the first to compel the shogunal government to open its doors. The betting, we might say, was on the Russians. For in October 1852, there set off from Europe on the long voyage to the Far

Excerpted from *A History of Modern Japan*, by Richard Storry. Copyright © Richard Storry, 1960. Reprinted by permission of Penguin Books, Ltd.

East the Russian Admiral Putyatin, empowered to persuade the Japanese to sign a commercial treaty. However, when the four vessels of Putyatin's expedition approached Nagasaki in August 1853, an American squadron under Commodore Matthew Perry had already presented what amounted to an ultimatum to the shogunate.

AMERICA FELT A NEED TO OPEN JAPAN

Perry had delivered a letter from President [Millard] Fillmore, requesting the opening of trade relations, and he had warned the Japanese that he would be back again in Yedo Bay [near Tokyo] the following year to receive their answer. And he told them that on his second visit he would arrive with a much larger squadron.

Four factors combined to stimulate American interest in Japan. These were the development of trade with China through Canton, the growth of the American whaling industry in the Pacific, the opening-up of California, symbolized by the Gold Rush of 1849, and the progress of steam navigation. The Great Circle Route, the shortest to China from the Pacific Coast of America, took vessels very close to, and often in sight of, the shores of Japan. But sailors looked at the distant coastline with some apprehension. It was known that for any seamen who happened to be stranded in Japan—and this was apt to occur to shipwrecked whaling crews from time to time—the treatment was unfriendly and disagreeable, although in general by no means intentionally cruel. The foreigners were minutely interrogated and then transported in closed palanquins—by reason of their size excruciatingly uncomfortable for other than Japanese passengers—all the way to Nagasaki, there to await eventual repatriation through the Dutch at Deshima.

Thus one of the purposes of Perry's expedition was to obtain a promise from the Japanese of future good treatment of any shipwrecked Americans. But although much play was made of this then, and in subsequent histories dealing with American-Japanese relations, it may be doubted whether the treatment of American nationals in Japan played more than a minor part in the motives behind Commodore Perry's visit to Japan in the summer of 1853. Of much more importance was, for example, the need to secure supplies, including coal, for American ships sailing to and from Canton. There was too, the expectation that a useful trade could be driven with the closed country, an expectation sharpened by the prospect of competition from Great Britain. Certain businessmen exerted considerable pressure in Washington towards the authorization of a naval expedition to force open the closed door across the Pacific. Nobody was more

Commodore Perry led the U.S. naval expedition to Japan in order to open trade between Japanese and Western nations.

active than a certain Aaron Haight Palmer, an energetic New York commission agent profoundly interested in the steamship trade with the Orient. Similar pressure on Congress came from churches, missionary boards, diplomats, and naval officers. Indeed the very development of transcontinental communications across the United States from the Middle West to the Pacific was closely related, in the eyes of many exuberant people at the time, with the vision of America becoming, as part of her 'manifest destiny', the commercial leader in both China and Japan. . . .

Perry's unbending firmness towards the Japanese was largely motivated by his knowledge of what had happened seven years earlier, when another American naval officer, Commodore Biddle, had tried to negotiate with the Japanese and had been repulsed. On that occasion Biddle had been bound by instructions from Washington to act cautiously; and accordingly he had been very conciliatory in his approach. This had been interpreted by the Japanese as weakness, with results unfavourable to American prestige. So Perry on his first visit simply handed over the President's letter to Japanese representatives on shore, having first refused to deal with the minor officials who were sent to him, and declared that he would return for an answer next year. Then, before departing, he sailed, in defiance of the Japanese, further up the Bay of Yedo to within sight of the suburbs of the city.

A THREAT JAPAN COULD NOT MEET

The 'Black Ships', as they were known, created a tremendous sensation on shore. There were, on this first visit in July 1853, four of them—two driven by steam. Most of the Japanese had never seen or imagined such ships. But the government in Yedo was not taken by surprise by this unwelcome visit. Plenty of warnings of a general nature had been received, through the Dutch, that some such expedition was on its way. Furthermore, information about Perry's squadron had reached Yedo from Okinawa, through Satsuma; for Perry was in the Ryukyus before coming to Japan, and it was in fact his full intention that advance news of his impending arrival should reach the Japanese authorities.

Perry's expedition, and of course Admiral Putyatin's of the same year, faced the shogunate with a most unpleasant dilemma. Quite apart from the laughable disparity between the military power of Japan and that of the great Western nations now pressing upon her, a disparity that would ensure the complete defeat of Japan if she chose to go to war, it was perfectly easy for a hostile fleet to impose starvation upon the inhabitants of Yedo, for the great bulk of the food supplies for the city came in from the north and west by sea. Interference with this traffic and with Japanese fishing vessels would have an effect on Yedo that would be both rapid and catastrophic. Serious resistance, then, was scarcely feasible.

CHARLES DARWIN DEFENDS HIS THEORY OF NATURAL SELECTION

CHARLES DARWIN

In 1859 the English naturalist Charles Darwin published *On the Origin of Species*, one of the most important scientific works in history. The work was the product of years of observation of natural life, much of which was undertaken on Darwin's voyage around the world on the H.M.S. *Beagle*. Darwin had concluded from his research that species were subject to a process he called natural selection, by which physical adaptations, produced by numerous slow and minute variations better suited organisms to their environment, thus ensuring propagation and survival. Darwin's was in fact the first concise and demonstrated statement of the theory of evolution. It has sparked controversy and inspired scientists ever since its initial publication.

In the following selection from the conclusion of his book, Darwin summarizes some of the main points of his argument, such as the unusual similarities among different species, which seem to imply an evolutionary connection, and defends his findings against the incorrect assumptions and inconsistent logic he expects to find among his scientific peers. He also suggests that his findings do not constitute a challenge to religious beliefs.

Excerpted from *The Origin of Species*, by Charles Darwin, 1859.

The fact, as we have seen, that all past and present organic beings can be arranged within a few great classes, in groups subordinate to groups, and with the extinct groups often falling in between the recent groups, is intelligible on the theory of natural selection with its contingencies of extinction and divergence of character. On these same principles we see how it is, that the mutual affinities of the forms within each class are so complex and circuitous. We see why certain characters are far more serviceable than others for classification;—why adaptive characters, though of paramount importance to the beings, are of hardly any importance in classification; why characters derived from rudimentary parts, though of no service to the beings, are often of high classificatory value; and why embryological characters are often the most valuable of all. The real affinities of all organic beings, in contradistinction to their adaptive resemblances, are due to inheritance or community of descent. The Natural System is a genealogical arrangement, with the acquired grades of difference, marked by the terms, varieties, species, genera, families, &c.; and we have to discover the lines of descent by the most permanent characters whatever they may be and of however slight vital importance.

SIMILARITIES AMONG SPECIES

The similar framework of bones in the hand of a man, wing of a bat, fin of the porpoise, and leg of the horse,—the same number of vertebrae forming the neck of the giraffe and of the elephant,— and innumerable other such facts, at once explain themselves on the theory of descent with slow and slight successive modifications. The similarity of pattern in the wing and in the leg of a bat, though used for such different purpose,—in the jaws and legs of a crab,—in the petals, stamens, and pistils of a flower, is likewise, to a large extent, intelligible on the view of the gradual modification of parts or organs, which were aboriginally alike in an early progenitor in each of these classes. On the principle of successive variations not always supervening at an early age, and being inherited at a corresponding not early period of life, we clearly see why the embryos of mammals, birds, reptiles, and fishes should be so closely similar, and so unlike the adult forms. We may cease marvelling at the embryo of an airbreathing mammal or bird having branchial slits and arteries running in loops, like those of a fish which has to breathe the air dissolved in water by the aid of well-developed branchiae.

Disuse, aided sometimes by natural selection, will often have reduced organs when rendered useless under changed habits or conditions of life; and we can understand on this view the mean-

ing of rudimentary organs. But disuse and selection will generally act on each creature, when it has come to maturity and has
to play its full part in the struggle for existence, and will thus
have little power on an organ during early life; hence the organ
will not be reduced or rendered rudimentary at this early age.
The calf, for instance, has inherited teeth, which never cut
through the gums of the upper jaw, from an early progenitor having well-developed teeth; and we may believe, that the teeth in
the mature animal were formerly reduced by disuse, owing to
the tongue and palate, or lips, having become excellently fitted
through natural selection to browse without their aid; whereas
in the calf, the teeth have been left unaffected, and on the principle of inheritance at corresponding ages have been inherited
from a remote period to the present day. On the view of each or-
ganism with all its separate parts having been specially created,
now utterly inexplicable is it that organs bearing the plain stamp
of inutility, such as the teeth in the embryonic calf or the shriv-
elled wings under the soldered wing-covers of many beetles,
should so frequently occur. Nature may be said to have taken
pains to reveal her scheme of modification, by means of rudimentary organs, of embryological and homologous structures,
but we are too blind to understand her meaning.

I have now recapitulated the facts and considerations which
have thoroughly convinced me that species have been modified,
during a long course of descent. This has been effected chiefly
through the natural selection of numerous successive, slight,
favourable variations; aided in an important manner, by the inherited effects of the use and disuse of parts; and in an unimportant manner, that is in relation to adaptive structures, whether
past or present, by the direct action of external conditions, and
by variations which seem to us in our ignorance to arise spontaneously. It appears that I formerly underrated the frequency and
value of these latter forms of variation, as leading to permanent
modifications of structure independently of natural selection. But
as my conclusions have lately been much misrepresented, and it
has been stated that I attribute the modification of species exclu-
sively to natural selection, I may be permitted to remark that in
the first edition of this work, and subsequently, I placed in a most
conspicuous position—namely, at the close of the Introduction—
the following words: "I am convinced that natural selection has
been the main but not the exclusive means of modification." This
has been of no avail. Great is the power of steady misrepresen-
tation; but the history of science shows that fortunately this
power does not long endure.

It can hardly be supposed that a false theory would explain, in so satisfactory a manner as does the theory of natural selection, the several large classes of facts above specified. It has recently been objected that this is an unsafe method of arguing; but it is a method used in judging of the common events of life, and has often been used by the greatest natural philosophers. The undulatory theory of light has thus been arrived at; and the belief in the revolution of the earth on its own axis was until lately supported by hardly any direct evidence. It is no valid objection that science as yet throws no light on the far higher problem of the essence or origin of life. Who can explain what is the essence of the attraction of gravity? No one now objects to following out the results consequent on this unknown element of attraction; notwithstanding that Leibnitz formerly accused Newton of introducing "occult qualities and miracles into philosophy."

Natural Selection Is Not a Challenge to Religion

I see no good reason why the views given in this volume should shock the religious feelings of any one. It is satisfactory, as showing how transient such impressions are, to remember that the greatest discovery ever made by man, namely, the law of the attraction of gravity, was also attacked by Leibnitz, "as subversive of natural, and inferentially of revealed, religion." A celebrated author and divine has written to me that "he has gradually learnt to see that it is just as noble a conception of the Deity to believe that He created a few original forms capable of self-development into other and needful forms, as to believe that He required a fresh act of creation to supply the voids caused by the action of His laws."

Why, it may be asked, until recently did nearly all the most eminent living naturalists and geologists disbelieve in the mutability of species? It cannot be asserted that organic beings in a state of nature are subject to no variation; it cannot be proved that the amount of variation in the course of long ages is a limited quality; no clear distinction has been, or can be, drawn between species and well-marked varieties. It cannot be maintained that species when intercrossed are invariably sterile, and varieties invariably fertile; or that sterility is a special endowment and sign of creation. The belief that species were immutable productions was almost unavoidable as long as the history of the world was thought to be of short duration; and now that we have acquired some idea of the lapse of time, we are too apt to assume, without proof, that the geological record is so perfect that it would have afforded us plain evidence of the mutation of species, if they had undergone mutation.

But the chief cause of our natural unwillingness to admit that one species has given birth to clear and distinct species, is that we are always slow in admitting great changes of which we do not see the steps. The difficulty is the same as that felt by so many geologists, when Lyell first insisted that long lines of inland cliffs had been formed, the great valleys excavated, by the agencies which we see still at work. The mind cannot possibly grasp the full meaning of the term of even a million years; it cannot add up and perceive the full effects of many slight variations, accumulated during an almost infinite number of generations.

Although I am fully convinced of the truth of the views given in this volume under the form of an abstract, I by no means expect to convince experienced naturalists whose minds are stocked with a multitude of facts all viewed, during a long course of years, from a point of view directly opposite to mine. It is so easy to hide our ignorance under such expressions as the "plan of creation," "unity of design," &c., and to think that we give an explanation when we only re-state a fact. Any one whose disposition leads him to attach more weight to unexplained difficulties than to the explanation of a certain number of facts will certainly reject the theory. A few naturalists, endowed with much flexibility of mind, and who have already begun to doubt the immutability of species, may be influenced by this volume; but I look with confidence to the future,—to young and rising naturalists, who will be able to view both sides of the question with impartiality. Whoever is led to believe that species are mutable will do good service by conscientiously expressing his conviction; for thus only can the load of prejudice by which this subject is overwhelmed be removed.

OTHER NATURALISTS' CONCLUSIONS ARE INCONSISTENT

Several eminent naturalists have of late published their belief that a multitude of reputed species in each genus are not real species; but that other species are real, that is, have been independently created. This seems to me a strange conclusion to arrive at. They admit that a multitude of forms, which till lately they themselves thought were special creations, and which are still thus looked at by the majority of naturalists, and which consequently have all the external characteristic features of true species,—they admit that these have been produced by variation, but they refuse to extend the same view to other and slightly different forms. Nevertheless they do not pretend that they can define, or even conjecture, which are the created forms of life, and which are those produced by secondary laws. They admit variation as a *vera causa* [true cause] in one case, they arbitrarily reject it in another, without assigning any distinction in the two cases. The day will come when this will be given as a curious illustration of the blindness of preconceived opinion. These authors seem no more startled at a miraculous act of creation than at an ordinary birth. But do they really believe that at innumerable periods in the earth's history certain elemental atoms have been commanded suddenly to flash into living tissues? Do they believe that at each supposed act of creation one individual or many were produced? Were all the infinitely numerous kinds of animals and plants created as eggs or seed, or as full grown? and in the case of mammals, were they created bearing the false marks of nourishment from the mother's womb? Undoubtedly some of these same questions cannot be answered by those who believe in the appearance or creation of only a few forms of life, or of some one form alone. It has been maintained by several authors that it is as easy to believe in the creation of a million beings as of one; but Maupertuis' philosophical axiom "of least action" leads the mind more willingly to admit the smaller number; and certainly we ought not to believe that innumerable beings within each great class have been created with plain, but deceptive, marks of descent from a single parent.

As a record of a former state of things, I have retained in the foregoing paragraphs, and elsewhere, several sentences which imply that naturalists believe in the separate creation of each species; and I have been much censured for having thus expressed myself. But undoubtedly this was the general belief when the first edition of the present work appeared. I formerly spoke to very many naturalists on the subject of evolution, and never once met with any sympathetic agreement. It is probable that some did then believe in evolution, but they were either silent, or expressed themselves so ambiguously that it was not easy to understand their meaning. Now things are wholly changed, and almost every naturalist admits the great principle of evolution. There are, however, some who still think that species have suddenly given birth, through quite unexplained means, to new and totally different forms: but, as I have attempted to show, weighty evidence can be opposed to the admission of great and abrupt modifications. Under a scientific point of view, and as leading to further investigation, but little advantage is gained by believing that new forms are suddenly developed in an inexplicable manner from old and widely different forms, over the old belief in the creation of species from the dust of the earth.

THE CAUSES OF THE AMERICAN CIVIL WAR WERE COMPLEX

BRUCE COLLINS

In the following selection Bruce Collins asserts that the American Civil War, a very destructive conflict fought from 1861 to 1865, can be understood in a number of ways. Rather than a relatively simple conflict to free America's southern slaves, the war instead reflected two different ways of life. While the North was by 1861 developing an urban, industrialized economy, the South remained rural and agrarian. Moreover, as Collins notes, contemporaries such as Abraham Lincoln described the war as a conflict between brothers as well as an attempt to preserve the American Union.

Adding further complexity to the understanding of the Civil War is the fact, Collins claims, that it inspired long-term hostility and misunderstanding between North and South. Both sides have told the Civil War story according to their own perspectives.

Bruce Collins is professor of American history at the University of Glasgow in Scotland.

At first glance the American Civil War seems a straightforward affair. Compared with the other major civil wars that have affected Western man, America's conflict has a pleasing simplicity. Geographical lines fairly clearly divided the two sides; the slave states of the South fought the free states of the North with a handful of border states caught divided in between. The American Civil War did not apparently spawn the complex ideological disputes and bizarre, exotic radical groups that have arisen in some of Europe's revolutionary struggles. Nor did the American Civil War involve the various rises, falls, and subdivisions of aristocratic and middle classes which are the stuff of European domestic upheavals. Yet few Americans at the time believed that their differences were clear-cut or simply defined.

Americans initially disagreed over what to call the events that afflicted them for the four years following 15 April 1861. For many Northerners, they constituted simply the Great Rebellion or the War for the Union; officially they were part of the War of the Rebellion. For leading Northerners, the fighting meant different things. Horace Greeley, a prominent Northern newspaper editor, saw the war as the American Conflict; President Lincoln emphasized that it was 'a people's contest' with republican and democratic government at stake; one of his party colleagues, Senator Henry Wilson, later wrote his account of the years from the 1840s to the 1860s and entitled it *History of the Rise and Fall of the Slave Power in America.* To Southerners, different names seemed appropriate. When the Confederate president Jefferson Davis wrote his memoirs he placed his emphasis on the Confederacy itself, on the attempt to create a new government; when his vice-president, Alexander H. Stephens, did the same he called his book *A Constitutional View of the Late War between the States;* and a modern historian has aptly referred to the War for Southern Independence.

These differences of nomenclature suggest deeper disagreements over the nature of the crisis that confronted Americans in the 1860s. Did Northerners fight Southerners simply to maintain the Union? Did Southerners fight as a self-conscious, fully fledged nation for an independence based on constitutional right; or were they led disingenuously into revolution by the so-called Slave Power, the slaveowning élite? Was the war a clash between two peoples, or a sectional rebellion by the Southern states brought about either by class interests or by widely resented Northern infringements of Southerners' rights? At the time, then, the war was variously interpreted; not surprisingly, its origins have been much discussed and disputed ever since.

THE FIRST "MODERN" WAR

The Civil War was a great explosion in nineteenth-century America. It was one of the most bloody major wars fought by 'Western man' before the twentieth century; from a population of 31 million in 1861, at least 600,000 people died as a result of the war. It is often regarded as the first 'modern' war: vast conscript armies were used; railways provided previously unattainable military mobility; campaigns of prolonged attrition in Virginia foreshadowed the mauling process that was Europe's Western Front in 1914–18; and, when the Northern breakthrough into the heartland of the Confederacy occurred, the civilian population in parts of the South experienced the novel ugliness of 'total' war.

Nor did conflict end in 1865. Most confederate states were occupied by federal forces for much of the period until 1870–2 and three of them remained subject in part to Northern rule until 1877. The war also left deep psychological wounds. The sectional antagonism existing before 1861 degenerated further into a deep-grained, bitter hatred felt by Southerners towards Yankees and the North after 1865. Southerners, uniquely among Americans until the Vietnam war, bore the stigma of military defeat and moral obloquy. Not until the 1960s did a genuine easing of sectional tensions begin to erase the memory of what white Southerners continued to call the War between the States. Historians have therefore rightly pondered the reasons why a war so long, intense, and bloody, whose psychological effects have been so persistently and keenly felt, came about.

Historians' perspectives on the origins of the war are shaped to an extent impossible to estimate by their assessment of its impact on American development. Many have seen the Civil War as a positive contribution to American progress. For some, it resulted in the triumph of industrialism and modernity over agrarianism and a semi-feudal order. This victory may not be desirable, but it is an inevitable part of Western social progression. For many, the war vindicated American morality and advanced American notions of civil rights; John Stuart Mill, pre-eminent English political economist of the mid-nineteenth century, found something to respect in the nation of 'dollar-hunters' when Northerners resisted the Slave Power and destroyed slavery. And for many Northerners, it consolidated a great nation and quashed an attempt to fragment that nation. Yet to many contemporaries—including, notably, Abraham Lincoln—the war was an unfortunate, indeed tragic, result of fraternal misunderstanding.

EUROPEAN POWERS INVADE MEXICO

LONDON MORNING POST

In the early 1860s, while the United States was in the throes of the Civil War and unable to enforce the Monroe Doctrine, a coalition of Great Britain, France, and Spain mounted an invasion of Mexico. The prime mover behind the invasion was Napoléon III, the emperor of France, who wanted a triumph to shore up his evaporating support at home and to limit the growing domination of the Americas by the United States. As the following article from London's *Morning Post* indicates, the British approved of the invasion. According to the newspaper, the invasion would bring the benefits of European civilization to the Mexicans as well as open Mexico to European colonialism and economic activity.

The French succeeded in conquering Mexico and for a short time installed a puppet emperor, Maximilian, on the throne. In 1867, however, they were finally defeated by a combination of American pressure and a Mexican nationalist army led by Benito Juarez. Mexico still celebrates as a national holiday an early victory in the war against the French, the Battle of Puebla, on May 5, 1862.

We have reason to believe that it is no longer premature to congratulate the civilised world on the vigorous character which the allied Mexican intervention has assumed, and on the understandings which have been arrived at for the future government of Mexico. By the common consent of the three intervening Powers it has been thought impossible to limit the present intervention to transactions of an indemnificatory nature on the coast, which, though effectual for their imme-

From the *London Morning Post*, February 4, 1862.

diate object, would offer no permanent guarantee for the restoration of the country to that social security and political stability which we all desire that it should enjoy.

EUROPEAN POWERS DISAPPROVED OF MEXICO'S RULERS

It can have escaped no one that the de facto depositaries of power in Mexico are little better than an organised association of rival brigands, who are the worst tyrants by which almost any people have ever been afflicted, and from whom the Mexicans themselves, whether Spanish or Indian, are praying to be delivered. These ostensibly hostile generals appear to be governed all the while by an excellent understanding between themselves, under which each has his share in domestic spoil. The people meantime are debarred, by the violence of their present rulers, from any free manifestation of their opinions. But it is clear that a republican policy is quite unsuited to the interests of all classes; and the dominant nationality in Mexico is of that Spanish blood which has nearly always supported the principle of monarchical government. The faithlessness of the existing authorities of Mexico, both to treaties and to public law, having placed England, France, and Spain at war with them, it becomes simply a matter of pol-

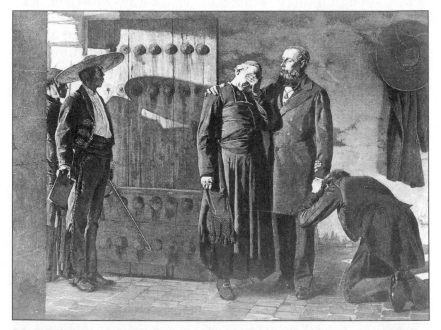

Maximilian is pictured above in resignation as the Mexican nationalist army terminates his reign. Despite France's early success in conquering Mexico, their rule ended in 1867.

icy and arrangement between the allies to what extent their intervention shall extend. We understand that it has now been determined (with the assent of Great Britain) by the Courts of Paris and Madrid that their armies shall march direct from Vera Cruz to the capital of Mexico, and there suppress an Executive even more tyrannous to its own fellow-citizens than faithless to the European Powers. . . .

INSTALLING A EUROPEAN EMPEROR: MAXIMILIAN

We believe that it is a probable result of this march of the allies on Mexico that that unhappy and distracted republic will reappear to the world as a constitutional monarchy, and that the Archduke Maximilian, brother of Francis-Joseph, Emperor of Austria, will assume the title of King of Mexico. At present, indeed, the Mexicans are really without a constitution. It would be a misapplication of terms to call the clique of usurpers who have been successively ruling, or rather grinding down, that people as in any sense a Government. The republican constitution has, in point of fact, been long annulled. The inevitable result of the advance of the allies is the fall of the existing tyranny. The people must then be consulted. And when we say the people, we can hardly go further than the European or semi-European races. There is every reason to believe that this community will cheerfully and thankfully receive a constitutional Sovereign presented to them by the common voice of their deliverers. They have tried a republic, and it has sunk away under a succession of atrocious military tyrannies. They are believed to be convinced that a monarchy will give them order, and that a constitutional monarchy will ensure them the only freedom they can possibly maintain. We believe that the Archduke Maximilian, both by character and by descent, will prove just the sort of prince that the Mexicans would desire. He is understood to be a Liberal Catholic—a follower of the religious belief of his family, and inclined in politics to the wise and moderate counsels of his astute relative by marriage, the present King of the Belgians. This is certainly the sort of monarch for a Catholic people who wish to be free. The Archduke Maximilian is also the direct descendant of the Emperor Charles V, who was King of Spain and the Indies, and of Ferdinand and Isabella, the founders of the transatlantic dominion of Spain. He is, moreover, collaterally descended from all the German Kings of Spain, from the accession of Philip II in 1556, to the death of Charles II in 1700. The present ruling family, indeed, who acceded to the throne of Spain only in the age of its decrepitude, with the accession of Philip V in the last-named year, are not associated with any of the traditions of Spanish colonisation in Mexico. It will not impossibly be found necessary to maintain an army of occupation in support of the new Government until it shall have derived sufficient stability to stand alone. Meanwhile, we shall of course pursue our original scheme of indemnification at the ports on the Gulf.

MEXICO'S GREAT POTENTIAL

There is no doubt that Mexico may yet be the most prosperous country in the world. She has five times the area of France, a soil incomparably more fertile, with the widest variations of temperature and climate in the different districts. We think it extremely probable that Mexico may yet become a field for extensive European colonisation. Not only have the dominating race been Europeans for four centuries, but it is a singular fact that nearly every valuable animal not *feræ naturæ* [indigenous] is of European importation. The high tableland, forming the bulk of the area of the country, has a perpetual soft spring temperature; and indeed there is every variety of mean heat, from the hot coast and to the icy tops of the Cordilleras. The plains are well suited to the growth of cotton, as well as to that of sugar and indigo. The foreign trade of Vera Cruz alone has averaged thirty or forty million dollars yearly. But it may be taking too distant a view to enter at present on such a prospect as the productive future of Mexico. We must content ourselves for the present with a contemplation of the political changes likely to be brought about in a country which has hitherto been one of the richest by nature and one of the poorest by misgovernment.

National Unity and Technological Change

CHAPTER 2

THE WORLD CELEBRATES THE OPENING OF THE SUEZ CANAL

ARNOLD T. WILSON

In the following selection Arnold T. Wilson, an officer in Great Britain's colonial service, describes the events surrounding the opening of the Suez Canal in 1869. The canal, one of the great commercial and engineering accomplishments of the nineteenth century, made rapid transportation between Europe and Asia possible by connecting the Mediterranean Sea with the Red Sea and the Indian Ocean.

The canal ran through Egyptian territory, nominally part of the Turkish Ottoman Empire. Realizing the commercial and political advantages to be gained by digging the canal, a French-Egyptian consortium began construction in 1859 with the backing of the French emperor Napoléon III and the Turkish sultan Ismail Pasha. The guiding light behind the canal was Ferdinand de Lesseps, a French diplomat whom Wilson describes as nervous yet confident as his ship, *l'Aigle,* led other ships on the first journey by water from the Mediterranean to the Red Sea.

Arnold T. Wilson was the author of numerous works on Middle Eastern and Iranian history.

Excerpted from *The Suez Canal: Its Past, Present, and Future,* by Arnold T. Wilson (Oxford: Oxford University Press, 1933). Reprinted by permission of Oxford University Press.

On 19th March 1869, in the presence of the Khedive [the Egyptian leader], the Prince and Princess of Wales, and a brilliant company of Egyptian notables and foreign visitors, the canal sluices were opened to admit into the Bitter Lakes, the ancient Gulf of Heroöpolis, several feet below sea-level, the waters of the Mediterranean. The filling required fifteen hundred million cubic metres of water and was not complete till 24th October. Once full, a single barrier beyond Chalouf was all that restrained the further progress of the water. Final completion of the canal was now in sight, and [canal designer Ferdinand] de Lesseps, whose genius for organization comprehended, as will have been gathered from the preceding pages, the use of publicity on a grand scale now gave notice that the canal would be formally opened on 17th November 1869. For four days the vessels would be permitted to pass free of charge and, thereafter, upon payment of the published dues. This announcement was supplemented by personal invitations to most of the reigning sovereigns of Europe by [Turkish sultan] Ismaïl Pasha, who was making a grand tour of Europe. Never did de Lesseps display greater boldness than in fixing this early date for the inauguration of the principal work of his life: the unexpected obstacles remained till the last moment, but melted before his foresight and courage, and before the skill of his executive staff and the devotion of the whole corps of labourers.

THREATS TO THE CANAL

On 2nd November between two soundings, taken at a distance of 130 metres, by means of square shafts holding twelve men, a hard rock was discovered, which broke the buckets of the dredger. It was 5 metres above the bottom of the canal. 'Every one', said de Lesseps afterwards, 'began by declaring there was nothing to be done: "Go and get powder in Cairo"—said I—"powder in masses—and then, if we cannot blow up the rock we will blow ourselves up. The intelligence and energy of our workmen saved us. From the beginning of the work there was not a tent-keeper who did not consider himself an agent of civilization. Hence our success."

On the night of 15th November a fire broke out at Port Said among the fireworks destined for the fêtes [opening-day celebrations]. They had been placed in a timberyard in the middle of the town. Only the timely arrival of 2,000 troops saved the town for, buried hard-by in the sand, lay a great quantity of gunpowder.

On the 16th an abnormally high tide covered the ground destined for the opening ceremony and surrounded the platforms: with difficulty was dry ground made for the visitors. The same

evening the *Latif,* an Egyptian frigate, ran aground in the canal,
thirty kilometres from Port Said. All efforts to dislodge her failed.
The [Khedive] repaired to the scene with 1,000 men. 'We agreed',
said de Lesseps, 'that there were three methods to be employed—
to float her, to beach her on one bank, or—"Blow it up", cried the
Prince. "Yes, yes, that's it—It will be magnificent," and I embraced
him. Next morning I went on board the *Aigle* [de Lessep's ship:
the first through the canal] without mentioning the accident. I did
not wish to change the programme. Logically I was wrong; the results proved me right. We must not be *doctrinaires* [too bound by
our original plan]. It answers neither in business nor in politics.
Five minutes only before reaching the scene I learned by signal
that the canal was free, and the brave little *Latif* intact.'

'Within the cabin sat the [French] Empress Eugénie, a prey to
the most grievous emotions: every moment she thought she saw
the *Aigle* stop, the honour of the French flag compromised, our
labours lost. Overcome by her feelings she left the company, and
we overheard her sobs—sobs which do her honour—for it was
French patriotism overflowing from her heart.' The risk he ran
was the measure of his success. 'The canal', he said in a lecture in
April, 1870, 'was indeed opened on 17th November, but not without terrible emotions. I have never seen so clearly how near is fail-

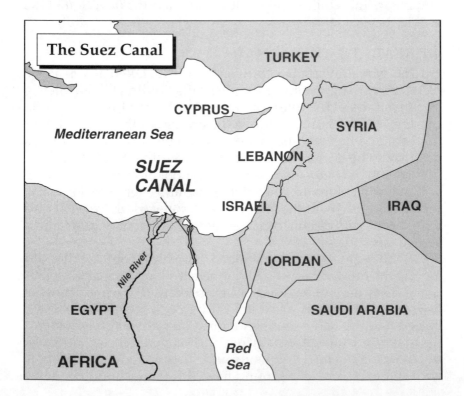

ure to triumph, but, at the same time, that triumph belongs to him who, marching onward, places his confidence in God and man.' On 17th November the channel was open, and the marriage of the two oceans was celebrated by the slow passage, lasting three days, of the Government fleet through the new waterway.

ROYAL OBSERVERS AND RELIGIOUS BLESSINGS

Sir Ian Malcolm thus describes the scene of de Lesseps' triumph:

> The little harbour at Port Saïd was alive with the ships of many nations, bearing the most eminent representatives of art and science, of commerce and industry, Sovereigns, Princes and Ambassadors, to enjoy the unbounded hospitality of the Khedive and to see with their own eyes this great thing that had actually come to pass. Already on November 13th, His Highness the Khedive had anchored his yacht the *Mahroussa* outside Port Saïd to receive his guests, whose arrivals from over many seas continued for three days and three nights: the Emperor of Austria, the Crown Prince of Prussia, members of other reigning families and finally the Empress Eugénie on board the *Aigle*. It was a gorgeous and a glittering scene at the doorway of the desert, there were fifty men-of-war flying the flags of all nations of Europe, firing salutes, playing their bands, whilst the sandy littoral was covered with tented Arabs and Beduin from far and near who had come with their families, on horseback and camel to join in the greatest festival that Egypt had seen since the days of the Ptolemies. On the foreground were erected three large pavilions or enclosed terraces; in the centre one were massed the illustrious guests of the Khedive; on the right hand was the Muhammadan hierarchy supported by its faithful, and on the left an altar for Christian worship and thanksgiving. When the rites of all the Churches had been duly celebrated and the Canal blessed, the Civil opening took place in official form. That evening (16th November) there was a display of fireworks, and festivities were prolonged far into the night. . . .

The festivities were not restricted to the canal zone. The present roadway leading between rows of trees from Cairo to the Pyramids was built, in the incredibly short time of six weeks, for the convenience of the [Khedive's] royal guests, by forced labour urged on by the lash. Verdi composed an opera, *Aïda*, specially for the occasion. It was magnificently presented at Cairo: all the

jewels worn on the stage, to the value of several millions, are reputed to have been real.

Great Britain, who almost alone of the Great Powers had
steadfastly obstructed the accomplishment of the project, was not
backward in offering honourable amends. De Lesseps received
at the hands of Queen Victoria the Grand Cross of the Star of India. The Lord Mayor of London, proposing his health at an official banquet in his honour, declared that 'our eminent engineers
made a mistake—M. de Lesseps was right, and the Suez Canal is
a living fact'. He was made a freeman of the City of London, and
the Prince of Wales, in presenting a Gold Medal to him at the
Crystal Palace, said:

> Great Britain will never forget that it is to you alone
> that we owe the success of this great achievement. . . .
> I hope that since you have been in our midst, our
> people have shown you how highly they appreciate
> the advantages that your splendid work has bestowed,
> and will continue to bestow upon our country.

THE UNIFICATION OF ITALY WAS A TRIUMPH OF BOTH NATIONALISM AND LIBERALISM

BENEDETTO CROCE

Nationalism and liberalism were among the most important movements in European society in the 1800s. Nationalism helped turn nineteenth-century Europe into a continent of competitive and creative nation-states. The goals of liberalism in that era included the spread of political rights to almost all peoples rather than a narrow group of nobles, churchmen, and soldiers.

In the following selection, philosopher and historian Benedetto Croce asserts that the unification of Italy, mostly completed in 1864, was perhaps the greatest liberal nationalist effort of the century, a masterpiece, as he puts it, of the political arts. Early in the century as well as in centuries past, Italy was made up of small independent kingdoms and city-states. Yet thanks to the efforts of the liberal monarch Victor Emmanuel, the astute politician Camille Cavour, and the people's revolutionary Giuseppe Garibaldi, Italians forged a movement called the Risorgimento, or rebirth. The Risorgimento created a liberal and democratic Italy that even conservative states such as Russia, which was still dominated by an absolute ruler and small aristocracy, recognized.

Benedetto Croce was an important Italian philosopher and historian of the early twentieth century.

Excerpted from *History of Europe in the Nineteenth Century,* by Benedetto Croce (New York: Harcourt, Brace, and World, 1933). Copyright Benedetto Croce Estate. Published in Italy by Adelphi Edizioni, Milano. Reprinted with permission from Harcourt.

I f it were possible in political history to speak of masterpieces as we do in dealing with works of art, the process of Italy's independence, liberty, and unity would deserve to be called the masterpiece of the liberal-national movements of the nineteenth century: so admirably does it exhibit the combination of its various elements, respect for what is old and profound innovation, the wise prudence of the statesmen and the impetus of the revolutionaries and the volunteers, ardour and moderation; so flexible and coherent is the logical thread by which it developed and reached its goal. It was called the Risorgimento, just as men had spoken of a rebirth of Greece, recalling the glorious history that the same soil had witnessed; but it was in reality a birth, a *sorgimento,* and for the first time in the ages there was born an Italian state with all and with only its own people, and moulded by an ideal. [King] Victor Emmanuel II was right when he said, in his speech from the throne on April 2, 1860, that Italy was no longer the Italy of the Romans or of the Middle Ages, but "the Italy of the Italians."

THE PAPACY OPPOSED ITALIAN UNIFICATION

Nor was this character, at once bold and moderate, lacking in the work of legislative and administrative and economic and financial construction of the new unitary state, which was carried out by excellent parliamentary work, principally between 1860 and 1865. And the enthusiasm was shown especially by the determination to solve the problem of the temporal power of the Papacy, of which the last but most precious remnant remained in Rome, and which was equally offensive to the national principle, as a wedge in the midst of the new state, and to the liberal consciousness, as incapable of change to civilized government. That the Papacy did not give in to these obvious national and civil arguments could not be a cause for astonishment, because the Church, a perfect society, embraces the temporal with the spiritual, and in her day extended her power far and wide, and invested and crowned the princes of the earth and excommunicated and deposed them, and if she now beheld herself reduced to ruling over a single fragment of Italy, had not for that reason given up a right that she was unable to give up without at the same time contradicting her own doctrine and nature. Not equally reasonable, nor altogether exempt from hypocrisy, were those Catholics, citizens of other states, who furiously defended the relic of temporal power in Rome—notably those French priests and bishops who used against Italy the eloquence of their pulpits as well as the attacks of their newspapers—because, in the last resort, they demanded that one single people should accomplish a duty which belonged to all Catholic peoples equally. They expected, with unchristian injustice, this one people to sacrifice its vital principles, which neither French nor Belgians nor Germans had ever sacrificed. But even in the Papacy, except for its doctrinal premises and traditional formulas, the spirit of a Gregory VII and an Innocent III was no longer alive, and least of all in Pius IX, of whom it was said that he was decidedly lukewarm about the political thesis that he was obliged to sustain until the end by every sort of means. In diplomatic circles it was told during these years that after listening to and accepting, with the expression demanded by the occasion, the condolences and protests conveyed to him by a great German personage because of the Italian onslaughts, he had turned to someone who was standing beside him and murmured: "This German imbecile does not understand the greatness and beauty of the Italian national idea!" . . .

ITALIAN LEADERS SET AN EXAMPLE FOR OTHERS

The Italian Risorgimento had been accompanied by the sympathy, the anxiety, and the admiration of the whole civilized world. The men who guided and impersonated it in the two years of the miracle, Victor Emmanuel [the future king of Italy], Cavour [the diplomat], Garibaldi [popular revolutionary leader], made a strong impression on men's imaginations, like everything that is great and extraordinary, but they also spoke to men's hearts because their significance was lifted above the particular passion of a people and stirred mankind—particularly in [Garibaldi,] the the poetic figure of the fighter in [Latin] America, the defender of Rome, the captain of the Thousand, on whose lips the brotherhood of peoples, the peace of the nations in liberty, justice, and harmonious labour, seemed to be a living reality. To the peoples that were still labouring in difficulties and conflicts similar to those which the Italians, after so many hindrances, obstacles, and disappointments, had happily overcome, to the Germans and the Hungarians and the Poles and the other Slavs, the Italian example appeared, as may well be imagined, as a lesson, a stimulus, a renewal of sorrow, a hope, an impulse to action. The revolutionary Bakunin, echoing what they all felt and thought, wrote at this time in one of his manifestos that "from Italy's victory over Austria dated the existence in Europe of a number of nations anxious for their liberty and capable of creating a new civilization founded upon liberty." In addition to this, the fall of the old political system, in the very country where Emperor and Pope and Bourbon and Lorraine princes clung fast together in order to maintain it, and the formation of the new kingdom without disorders and revenges or other shameful and cruel things (for, as

Cavour had said, liberty scorns the use in her favour of "the arms of despotism") shook the convictions of the refractory, calmed fears, relieved all tension, persuaded opponents not to persist in unwise denials, and inclined everyone to conciliation and to looking upon the liberal system with new eyes. The kingdom of Italy was recognized by the other states, even by those which were particularly conservative and authoritarian; as it was by Prussia as soon as the new king, William I, had overcome his instinctive reluctance, and in Russia by the son of Czar Nicholas, who would never have conceived the possibility of such a happening or of such recognition.

JAPAN REALIZES IT NEEDS WESTERN IDEAS

AKIRA IRIYE

After Japan was forced to open trade and diplomacy to the West by the United States in 1853, many Japanese realized they needed to control Western influence or be dominated by the West. To that end, and believing that the Tokugawa shoguns who had ruled Japan since 1603 were too weak in relation to the West, reformers overthrew the Tokugawa in 1868 and installed a new emperor, the Meiji emperor, who promised to support them.

   In the following selection, Akira Iriye describes some of the important ideas behind the "Meiji Restoration" (1868–1912), during which Japan grew capable of challenging the West militarily and economically. Iriye asserts that the Meiji reformers realized that Japan needed systems of government, bureaucracy, and education that emulated those found in such nations as Great Britain, the United States, and Germany.

   Akira Iriye is professor of American history at Harvard University.

T he Meiji Restoration of 1868 put an end to the reign of the Tokugawa shogunate (since the early seventeenth century) and established a new government under the emperor whose palace was moved to Tokyo, the new capital. By then a number of treaties had been signed with Western powers to regulate trade and other matters, and the new Meiji government started out by acknowledging the validity of these treaties. The

Excerpted from "The Origins of Modern Japanese Diplomacy," in *Japan and the Wider World*, by Akira Iriye (London: Longman). Copyright © Chuokoron-Sha, Inc., 1997. Reprinted with permission of Pearson Education Ltd.

powers, on their part, extended diplomatic recognition to Tokyo. But, even though Tokugawa officials had dealt with foreign affairs, the Meiji leaders had to learn much about the conduct of diplomacy, about international affairs in general, and, most fundamentally, about the West, its people and its culture.

A good example of this learning experience may be read in Iwakura Tomomi's exhortation to his countrymen in 1869: 'All human beings have horizontal eyes and vertical noses. Even if their hair is red and eyes blue, they are all human, endowed with their ideas of loyalty, filial piety, and marital affection. We should not despise them as barbarians but treat them as courteously as we would friends.' Iwakura, a court noble, was one of the young leaders of the Meiji government who, in 1871–73, led an embassy to the United States and Europe, the first official mission dispatched by the Meiji state. He, like his colleagues, was acutely aware of the need to appeal to his countrymen to overcome their anti-foreign prejudices, products of their over two hundred years' isolation from the rest of the world (except for China and the Netherlands, with which limited trade had been carried on even before the 1850s). Iwakura and other leaders knew that not only Japan's existence as an independent nation but also the very survival of the Meiji regime would be jeopardized if anti-foreign fanatics created incidents—as they had done during the decades preceding the Restoration—and brought about foreign intervention; that, too, had happened earlier in Japan and, as they were well aware, in China.

It is important to note that even at this early stage, Meiji leaders spoke of the need 'to protect the independence of the imperial nation' as the fundamental objective of their foreign policy. But how could such an objective be attained? Not, any longer, by maintaining a self-righteous isolation from world affairs or indulging in anti-foreign violence but by 'following the motions of the universe'. Diplomatic intercourse was seen as an inevitable 'motion' governing relations among nations, and Japan could not be excepted if it were to survive. But the Japanese knew that the 'universe' in this context essentially meant the Western powers. Whereas before the 1850s China had provided the mental universe in which affairs of state could be discussed, there was a quick shift of focus from China to the West. Having decided that international relations were, for all intents and purposes, those defined by the nations of Europe and North America, Tokyo's officials from early on tried to find out what lay behind the rise and growth of these countries' power and influence in the world.

What constituted a nation's power? How could it be augmented? It so happened that these questions, which European statesmen and scholars had been debating since the seventeenth century, were giving rise to some fresh perspectives and novel answers in the West during the 1870s, just when the Japanese were becoming obsessed with the issue of national independence. It may be said that this fortuitous circumstance facilitated Japan's quest for the secrets of the West's power. Japanese leaders like Iwakura and Ōkubo Toshimichi, perhaps the most powerful politician in the early Meiji period till he was assassinated in 1878, carefully observed Western nations during their world tour of 1871–73 and became convinced that ultimately the power of the Western nations derived from their modern political and economic systems: the coalescing of people's energies, the enhancing of their national consciousness through education, and the development of industry. Without such changes, mere military strengthening would not build national power. As they travelled to Europe and America, Iwakura, Ōkubo, and many others learned that the masses paid attention to national political affairs, that governments took pains to promote the welfare of the people. Government and people together then cooperated to enhance the power of the respective nations. Of course, the situation varied from country to country, and many other features distinguished Western nations, but the Meiji leaders were determined that political and economic reforms must take precedence over all others.

Such perceptions produced specific programmes for Japan's transformation. Politically, a constitutional monarchy patterned after the British and German examples was established, along with centralized systems of bureaucracy and education. These reforms could be undertaken without incurring too many diplomatic complications, but economic reforms were a different story. Without tariff autonomy, it was extremely difficult to develop indigenous industry; imported goods paid a minimum of customs duties, while exports had to be shipped abroad through the intermediary of foreign merchants residing in the open ports, where they enjoyed extraterritorial privileges. As Baba Tatsui, a political thinker who studied in Britain during the 1870s, wrote in 1876, so long as Western merchants enjoyed the unjust and improper privileges of extraterritoriality, Japan's commerce would only be destined to weaken and national wealth would be exhausted. Treaty revision was absolutely imperative if Japan were to strengthen its economic bases, not to mention upholding its national dignity. The government, sharing such views, was determined from early on to bring about the modification and ultimate abolition of the unequal treaties. 'Achieving equality with other nations', in the words of Sanjō Sanetomi, like Iwakura a court nobleman who occupied high posts in the early Meiji government, was thus considered an essential part of the programme for national strengthening.

At the back of such determination was a widely shared image of the West as a group of modernized nations. If Japan were to survive as an independent nation, it must be like them, politically and economically. Of course, this implied optimism that Japanese could undertake what the Westerners had accomplished. Modernization and Westernization were interchangeable. This was what Fukuzawa Yukichi, perhaps the most influential writer at that time, meant by his call for 'leaving Asia'; so long as Japan remained entrapped in traditional Asian ways, it could never achieve full independence. Japan could grow only if it 'marched alongside the civilized nations of the world', as he said. It should be noted that the West was not considered intrinsically either good or evil but was viewed pragmatically, as an object of emulation. The value lay not so much in the West as in the act of emulating the West. Westernization would not make Japan any more moral than it was, nor would it be used to oppose the West for some ulterior purposes. Modern transformation was not a moralistic proposition but rather an amoral (not necessarily immoral) prescription for national survival.

UNIFIED GERMANY TOOK ON PRUSSIAN OVERTONES

WILLIAM L. SHIRER

In the following selection, noted WWII historian and journalist William L. Shirer describes how the process of German unification was guided by the eastern German province of Prussia, thus giving Germany many Prussian values and characteristics. Prussia had turned itself into a major military power in the eighteenth century, Shirer asserts, but failed to develop a civilized, urban culture comparable to those of Britain and France. Its "Junker" nobles remained narrow-minded landlords and its peasants remained virtual slaves dedicated to supporting the nation's war machine. Even Otto von Bismarck, the Junker who carried out Germany's unification, failed to appreciate the civilized culture not only of Britain and France, but also of the rest of the German-speaking world.

Shirer argues that the German empire was no more than an "extension" of Prussia. Militarism and power were valued above all else, while democracy and individual rights were simply paid lip service. Nonetheless, many Germans were happy with this state of affairs since Bismarck's Prussian autocracy brought prosperity and glory to all Germany.

Journalist William L. Shirer lived in and reported on Germany in the 1920s and 1930s. He is the author of many memoirs and histories.

Beyond the Elbe to the east lay Prussia. As the nineteenth century waned, this century which had seen the sorry failure of the confused and timid liberals at Frankfurt in 1848–49 to create a somewhat democratic, unified Germany, Prussia took over the German destiny. For centuries this Germanic state had lain outside the main stream of German historical development and culture. It seemed almost as if it were a freak of history. Prussia had begun as the remote frontier state of Brandenburg on the sandy wastes east of the Elbe which, beginning with the eleventh century, had been slowly conquered from the Slavs. Under Brandenburg's ruling princes, the Hohenzollerns, who were little more than military adventurers, the Slavs, mostly Poles, were gradually pushed back along the Baltic. Those who resisted were either exterminated or made landless serfs. The imperial law of the German Empire forbade the princes from assuming royal titles, but in 1701 the Emperor acquiesced in the Elector Frederick III's being crowned King *in* Prussia at Koenigsberg.

By this time Prussia had pulled itself up by its own bootstraps to be one of the ranking military powers of Europe. It had none of the resources of the others. Its land was barren and bereft of minerals. The population was small. There were no large towns, no industry and little culture. Even the nobility was poor, and the landless peasants lived like cattle. Yet by a supreme act of will and a genius for organization the Hohenzollerns managed to create a Spartan military state whose well-drilled Army won one victory after another and whose Machiavellian diplomacy of temporary alliances with whatever power seemed the strongest brought constant additions to its territory.

PRUSSIA WAS ORGANIZED AROUND MILITARY FORCE

There thus arose quite artificially a state born of no popular force nor even of an idea except that of conquest, and held together by the absolute power of the ruler, by a narrow-minded bureaucracy which did his bidding and by a ruthlessly disciplined army. Two-thirds and sometimes as much as five-sixths of the annual state revenue was expended on the Army, which became, under the King, the state itself. "Prussia," remarked Mirabeau, "is not a state with an army, but an army with a state." And the state, which was run with the efficiency and soullessness of a factory, became all; the people were little more than cogs in the machinery. Individuals were taught not only by the kings and the drill sergeants but by the philosophers that their role in life was one of obedience, work, sacrifice and duty. Even [philosopher Immanuel] Kant preached that duty demands the suppression of human feeling, and the Prussian poet Willibald Alexis gloried in the enslavement of the people under the Hohenzollerns. To Lessing, who did not like it, "Prussia was the most slavish country of Europe."

The Junkers [Prussia's landowning nobles], who were to play such a vital role in modern Germany, were also a unique product of Prussia. They were, as they said, a master race. It was they who occupied the land conquered from the Slavs and who farmed it on large estates worked by these Slavs, who became landless serfs quite different from those in the West. There was an essential difference between the agrarian system in Prussia and that of western Germany and Western Europe. In the latter, the nobles, who owned most of the land, received rents or feudal dues from the peasants, who though often kept in a state of serfdom had certain rights and privileges and could, and did, gradually acquire their own land and civic freedom. In the West, the peasants formed a solid part of the community; the landlords, for all their drawbacks, developed in their leisure a cultivation which led to, among other things, a civilized quality of life that could be seen in the refinement of manners, of thought and of the arts.

The Prussian Junker was not a man of leisure. He worked hard at managing his large estate, much as a factory manager does today. His landless laborers were treated as virtual slaves. On his large properties he was the absolute lord. There were no large towns nor any substantial middle class, as there were in the West, whose civilizing influence might rub against him. In contrast to the cultivated *grand seigneur* [great nobleman] in the West, the Junker developed into a rude, domineering, arrogant type of man, without cultivation or culture, aggressive, conceited, ruthless, narrow-minded and given to a petty profit-seeking that some German historians noted in the private life of Otto von Bismarck, the most successful of the Junkers.

UNDER THE PRUSSIAN BISMARCK, GERMANY UNITES

It was this political genius, this apostle of "blood and iron," who between 1866 and 1871 brought an end to a divided Germany which had existed for nearly a thousand years and, by force, replaced it with Greater Prussia, or what might be called Prussian Germany. Bismarck's unique creation is the Germany we have known in our time, a problem child of Europe and the world for nearly a century, a nation of gifted, vigorous people in which first this remarkable man and then Kaiser Wilhelm II and finally Hitler, aided by a military caste and by many a strange intellectual, suc-

ceeded in inculcating a lust for power and domination, a passion
for unbridled militarism, a contempt for democracy and individual freedom and a longing for authority, for authoritarianism. . . .

"The great questions of the day," Bismarck declared on becoming Prime Minister of Prussia in 1862, "will not be settled by
resolutions and majority votes—that was the mistake of the men
of 1848 and 1849—but by blood and iron." That was exactly the
way he proceeded to settle them, though it must be said that he
added a touch of diplomatic finesse, often of the most deceitful
kind. Bismarck's aim was to destroy liberalism, bolster the power
of conservatism—that is, of the Junkers, the Army and the
crown—and make Prussia, as against Austria, the dominant
power not only among the Germans but, if possible, in Europe
as well. "Germany looks not to Prussia's liberalism," he told the
deputies in the Prussian parliament, "but to her force."

Bismarck first built up the Prussian Army and when the parliament refused to vote the additional credits he merely raised
them on his own and finally dissolved the chamber. With a
strengthened Army he then struck in three successive wars. The
first, against Denmark in 1864, brought the duchies of Schleswig
and Holstein under German rule. The second, against Austria in
1866, had far-reaching consequences. Austria, which for centuries
had been first among the German states, was finally excluded
from German affairs. It was not allowed to join the North German Confederation which Bismarck now proceeded to establish.

"In 1866," the eminent German political scientist Wilhelm
Roepke once wrote, "Germany ceased to exist." Prussia annexed
outright all the German states north of the Main which had
fought against her, except Saxony; these include Hanover, Hesse,
Nassau, Frankfurt and the Elbe duchies. All the other states north
of the Main were forced into the North German Confederation.
Prussia, which now stretched from the Rhine to Koenigsberg,
completely dominated it, and within five years, with the defeat
of Napoleon III's France, the southern German states, with the
considerable kingdom of Bavaria in the lead, would be drawn
into Prussian Germany.

Bismarck's crowning achievement, the creation of the Second
Reich, came on January 18, 1871, when King Wilhelm I of Prus-
sia was proclaimed Emperor of Germany in the Hall of Mirrors
at Versailles. Germany had been unified by Prussian armed force.
It was now the greatest power on the Continent; its only rival in
Europe was England.

Yet there was a fatal flaw. The German Empire, as Treitschke
said, was in reality but an extension of Prussia. "Prussia," he emphasized, "is the dominant factor. . . . The will of the Empire can

be nothing but the will of the Prussian state." This was true, and it was to have disastrous consequences for the Germans themselves. From 1871 to 1933 and indeed to Hitler's end in 1945, the course of German history as a consequence was to run, with the exception of the interim of the Weimar Republic, in a straight line and with utter logic.

Despite the democratic façade put up by the establishment of the Reichstag [Germany's Parliament], whose members were elected by universal manhood suffrage, the German Empire was in reality a militarist autocracy ruled by the King of Prussia, who was also Emperor. The Reichstag possessed few powers; it was little more than a debating society where the representatives of the people let off steam or bargained for shoddy benefits for the classes they represented. The throne had the power—by divine right. As late as 1910 Wilhelm II could proclaim that the royal crown had been "granted by God's Grace alone and not by parliaments, popular assemblies and popular decision. . . . Considering myself an instrument of the Lord," he added, "I go my way."

He was not impeded by Parliament. The Chancellor he appointed was responsible to him, not to the Reichstag. The assembly could not overthrow a Chancellor nor keep him in office. That was the prerogative of the monarch. Thus, in contrast to the development in other countries in the West, the idea of democracy, of the people sovereign, of the supremacy of parliament, never got a foothold in Germany, even after the twentieth century began. To be sure, the Social Democrats, after years of persecution by Bismarck and the Emperor, had become the largest single political party in the Reichstag by 1912. They loudly demanded the establishment of a parliamentary democracy. But they were ineffective. And, though the largest party, they were still a minority. The middle classes, grown prosperous by the belated but staggering development of the industrial revolution and dazzled by the success of Bismarck's policy of force and war, had traded for material gain any aspirations for political freedom they may have had. They accepted the Hohenzollern autocracy. They gladly knuckled under to the Junker bureaucracy and they fervently embraced Prussian militarism. Germany's star had risen and they—almost all the people—were eager to do what their masters asked to keep it high.

GERMANY'S RISE TO POWER IS A MIXED BLESSING

FREDERICK II

The unification of Germany in 1871 was one of the most important events of the nineteenth century, creating at a stroke a nation
able to challenge Great Britain, France, or any other state. The
movement to unify Germany, earlier a complicated collection of
city-states, kingdoms, and duchies, in part coincided with the
general nationalist trend of the age. But the process was carried
out under the guidance of the most powerful German state,
Prussia, and its prime minister, Otto von Bismarck, the so-called
Iron Chancellor, who adopted a policy he called "blood and
iron." Germany, Bismarck was sure, would be born out of military power, courage, and bloodshed, not political debate or the
democratic process. Consequently, Bismarck instigated victorious wars against Denmark, Austria, and France to establish Germany's place among European nations.

In the following selection, Frederick II, a Prussian prince
whose son later became the German emperor William II, wonders in his diary where Bismarck's policy will lead Germany if it
mostly inspires fear and hatred among other nations.

T he longer this struggle [the Franco-Prussian War of 1871]
lasts, the better for the enemy and the worse for us. The
public opinion of Europe has not remained unaffected by
the spectacle. We are no longer looked upon as the innocent suf-
ferers of wrong, but rather as the arrogant victors, no longer con-

Excerpted from Crown Prince Frederick II of Prussia's diary, in *The Age of Bismarck: Documents and Interpretations*, edited by Theodore Hamerow. Copyright © 1973 by Theodore
S. Hamerow. Reprinted by permission of HarperCollins Publishers, Inc.

tent with the conquest of the foe, but fain to bring about his utter ruin. No more do the French appear in the eyes of neutrals as
a mendacious, contemptible nation, but as the heroic-hearted
people that against overwhelming odds is defending its dearest
possessions in honourable fight. Nay, in their sympathy with
France men go so far as to hate Germany. In this nation of
thinkers and philosophers, poets and artists, idealists and enthusiasts, the world will recognize nothing but a people of con-
querors and destroyers, to which no pledged word, no treaty
concluded, is sacred, which speaks with rude insolence of others
that had done it no hurt and scornfully makes mock even of the
gifts offered it as tokens of sympathy and good will. Utterly false
as these views are, we cannot, unfortunately, deny their existence
and are bound to own that they are indeed well fitted to tarnish
the brightness of the good name we have hitherto enjoyed. True,
we are indisputably the foremost people of the world in civilization, yet at the moment it must seem as though we are neither
loved nor respected, but only feared. We are deemed capable of
every wickedness and the distrust felt for us grows ever more
and more pronounced. Nor is this the consequence of this war
only—so far has the theory, initiated by Bismarck and for years
holding the stage, of "Blood and Iron" brought us! What good to
us is all power, all martial glory and renown, if hatred and mis-
trust meet us at every turn, if every step we advance in our development is a subject for suspicion and grudging? Bismarck has
made us great and powerful, but he has robbed us of our friends,
the sympathies of the world, and—our conscience. I still hold fast
today to the conviction that Germany, without blood and iron,
simply by the justice of her cause, could make "moral conquests"
and, united, become free and powerful. A preponderance of quite
another kind than that gained by mere force of arms was within
our reach, for German culture, German science and German genius must have won us respect, love and—honor. . . .

The future holds for us the noble, but infinitely difficult task
of freeing the beloved German Fatherland from the baseless suspicion with which the world today regards her. We must prove
that the power acquired is not to beget dangers, but to bring with
it a blessing, the blessing of peace and civilization. But how hard
it will be to combat the worship of brute force and mere outward
success, to enlighten men's minds, to direct ambition and emulation once more to worthy and healthy objects! God grant it may
soon be possible to find the means to bring about an honorable
peace and put an end to useless bloodshed, before it has cost us
too excessive sacrifices! Even now the Bavarians, Saxons, and
Württembergers have suffered terribly, and the ranks of our of-

ficers are sadly dwindled, without any prospect of speedily filling the gaps. But at home the lofty spirit of holy, patriotic enthusiasm such as was shown in those unforgettable days of July, has
materially declined and given place to a feeling of discourage-
ment. Yet our gallant army bears all privations and sufferings
with unparalleled courage; to our soldiers and Fatherland we
owe it to be steadfast in patience and confidence and to face the
future with a strong heart and undaunted eyes. As the beginning
of the mighty war was fortunate beyond all hope and expectation, so must we in thankfulness and confidence trust that, in
spite of all changes and chances that may still befall, the end will
correspond with the beginning.

ALEXANDER GRAHAM BELL INVENTS THE TELEPHONE

ERNEST V. HEYN

The second half of the nineteenth century was a period of dramatic technological innovation. Building on earlier achievements in both technology and science, and convinced that new gadgets would yield great rewards, inventors produced such devices as the typewriter, the phonograph, the moving picture camera, and, as Ernest V. Heyn explains in the following selection, the telephone.

Heyn describes how Alexander Graham Bell, a Scottish engineer who moved to America, invented the telephone almost by mistake in his Boston laboratory in 1876. Bell went on to demonstrate the machine at the American Centennial Exhibition that same year, astounding even royalty with this machine that seemed to speak.

Ernest V. Heyn was editor-in-chief and associate publisher of the magazine *Popular Science Monthly*.

T he moment of discovery actually came on the sweltering afternoon of June 2, 1875, in a garret over the Williams electrical workshop. Bell in the receiving room and [his assistant Thomas] Watson in the transmitting room were patiently trying to overcome their harmonic telegraph's maddening foibles. The steel organ reeds (substituted for tuning forks) needed constant retuning by means of an adjustment screw. Sometimes, if a reed were screwed down too tightly, it stuck to the pole of the electromagnet beneath it instead of being free to vibrate. When

one of Watson's reeds, in the transmitting room, stopped vibrating, Watson plucked at it to free it, and as nothing happened,
kept on plucking it. An account of the day published in *Popular
Science* describes what happened next: "Suddenly there came a
shout from Bell and he rushed in excitedly from the next room.
'What did you do then? Don't change anything. Let me see!'"

A HAPPY ACCIDENT

Listening to the receiving reed at the other end of the line, Bell
heard a completely different sound from the usual transmitter
whine—the twang of a plucked reed complete with its timbre,
the complex set of tones and overtones that give character to
sound. He at once realized that the plucked reed, screwed down
too tightly to fulfill its normal, make-or-break, telegraphic function, had instead acted as a diaphragm, and sent continuous, but
fluctuating current over the line. In Watson's words: "The circuit
had remained unbroken while that strip of magnetized steel by
its vibration over the pole of its magnet was generating that mar-
velous conception of Bell's—a current of electricity that varied in
intensity precisely as the air was varying in density within hear-
ing distance of that spring. That undulatory current had passed
through the connecting wire to the distant receiver, which, fortunately, was a mechanism that could transform that current
back into an extremely faint echo of the sound of the vibrating
spring that had generated it, but what was still more fortunate,
the right man had that mechanism at his ear. . . . The speaking
telephone was born at that moment."

An accident. But, as [French biologist Louis] Pasteur once
wrote, "Chance favors the prepared mind." Everything in Bell's
background had prepared him for this chance brush with glory.
And he instantly seized the opportunity. Contrary to electrical
dogma, an induced electric current *could* be strong enough to be
useful. And surely he could devise diaphragms better suited to
speech than the steel reeds. "All the experimenting that followed
that discovery," says Watson, "up to the time the telephone was
put into practical use, was largely a matter of working out the details." Within days, the first, crude membrane diaphragm telephone transmitted the faint murmur of Bell's voice to Watson, although the words themselves couldn't be made out. It was not
until the following March—March 10, 1876—that Watson heard
"a complete and intelligible sentence." That was, of course, the
immortal "Mr. Watson, come here. I want you." In fact, whether
Bell actually spilled the now legendary battery acid, and whether,
indeed, these were the exact words Bell used, is totally, and im-
materially, uncertain. What is clear is that this model of the tele-

phone, one that used a battery and a variable resistance instead of a magneto transmitter, was the first really successful one. And a powered, variable-resistance transmitter made possible the enormous success of the future telephone industry. Three days before, Bell had received his first telephonic patent—possibly the most valuable patent in history.

The news of his discovery was soon broadcast in a way that could not have been better arranged by the most audacious of publicity agents. Again, happy coincidence smoothed the way. That year, 1876, was the year of the great Centennial Exhibition, held in Philadelphia and attended by notables from all over the world. Gardiner Hubbard, Bell's old friend, backer, and soon-to-be father-in-law, was one of three members of the committee on the Massachusetts science and education exhibit. He pressed Bell to participate; the result was that the state's exhibit included a table labeled "Telegraphic and Telephonic Apparatus By A. Graham Bell," which included both the variable-resistance and magnetic versions of the telephone. But Bell resisted going to the exhibition himself; he was immersed in school matters. Mabel, his fiancée, practically had to drag him to the railroad station, because he had, as he wrote his mother the next day, "not the remotest intention of leaving Boston." But, moved at seeing the young girl (she was eighteen) "pale and anxious," Bell got on the train. "What I am going to do in Philadelphia," he wrote, "I cannot tell."

In 1876 Alexander Graham Bell's invention of the telephone made its public debut at the Centennial Exhibition in Philadelphia.

What he did there is history. It is well described in the first in a remarkable series of *Popular Science* articles on the early telephone, written by Fred De Land starting in 1906. (Bell commented that the writer, whom he had never met, "seems to know more about me and what I have done than I know myself.")

Bell Amazes an Emperor

Sunday, June 25, 1876, was oppressively hot. It was the day a group of experts including the famous English scientist Sir William Thompson, later Lord Kelvin, was to judge the electrical exhibits. Bell's modest table was tucked in a remote corner of the sweltering exhibition building, by a flight of stairs, and before the moist and exhausted judges reached it they had run out of both time and energy. They probably would simply have not bothered, except that one of them recognized Bell, and insisted on seeing his exhibit. The fact that this person was Pedro II, the portly Emperor of Brazil, was probably of some influence with the other judges. Luckily, again, Dom Pedro had visited Bell at the Boston School for the Deaf just eleven days before, and had formed a warm impression of him. De Land writes: "His Majesty spoke so enthusiastically about the telephone, that, tired as the judges were, they concluded to investigate thoroughly its merits."

First, Sir William listened with the sheet-metal diaphragm of a receiver to his ear as Bell, at the far end of a gallery, sang and spoke into one of his electromagnetic transmitters. The first words Sir William clearly made out were "Do you understand what I say?" Amazed, he ran to tell Bell that he had indeed understood. When Dom Pedro took the receiver, he heard Bell reciting "To be or not to be," leaped from his chair, and shouted, "I hear, I hear," and soon Bell, still spouting Hamlet, saw Dom Pedro galumphing toward him at what he called "a very un-emperor-like gait."

Thomas Edison Had Ambitious Plans for Electric Power

ALAN I. MARCUS AND HOWARD P. SEGAL

Thomas Edison, who demonstrated a working lightbulb in 1879, is usually credited with the invention of the electric light. But, as Alan I. Marcus and Howard P. Segal suggest in the following selection, Edison's incandescent bulb was the product of both a public relations effort by Edison and the work of his team of inventors. Moreover, Edison built on the accomplishments of numerous scientists both prior to and contemporary with himself. He was no solitary tinkerer in his laboratory in Menlo Park, New Jersey, but rather, the authors suggest, a man who combined the skills of a clever engineer and organizer with those of a marketing genius.

Marcus and Segal go on to point out that Edison envisioned an entire electric power plant, not merely a lightbulb. His first plant, which opened in New York City in 1882, demonstrated that it was possible to distribute this amazing new source of light and power easily and inexpensively.

Alan I. Marcus is professor of history at Iowa State University. Howard P. Segal is professor of history at the University of Maine.

E dison had acquired a reputation as an inventor par excellence before he ever produced his first incandescent lamp. He had contributed to the "printing telegraph" (stock ticker), "speaking telegraph" (telephone), and "talking telegraph recorder" (phonograph). His youthful experience as a telegraph operator introduced him to shunts, relays, and continuous-feed belts (design elements Edison used repeatedly) and provided a rudimentary understanding of electrical principles such as Ohm's law. It also introduced him to investors familiar with electrical phenomena—telegraph investors. Edison parlayed their backing and his prominence to assemble an impressive staff of technical associates, and to stock extensive facilities. But Edison was not the first to investigate incandescent lighting. Several Europeans and Americans attempted in the two decades after 1840 to develop incandescent bulbs. Using electric batteries as power sources, these men sought to produce long-lasting filaments and vacuums strong enough to prevent combustion.

The inability to evacuate cylinders adequately doomed these early efforts. Not until after 1875 was an improved mercury air pump, developed a decade earlier by the German Herman Sprengel, employed in incandescent lighting work. Joseph Swan, a British pharmacist active in the mid-century lighting quest, was the first electrician to adapt the Sprengel pump, and he was soon joined by Americans Hiram Maxim, Moses Farmer, and others.

MARKETING THE ELECTRIC LIGHT

On one level, these investigators were Edison's competition. But he pursued incandescence from a different angle, one more nearly akin to the electrical efforts of [fellow inventors] Charles Brush, Edward Weston, and Elihu Thomson. Edison did not explore the possibility of incandescence; he did not begin by developing a lamp. He simply assumed that incandescence was possible and moved to the twin issues of marketability and practicality. Edison understood that success depended on incandescence's ability to supplant gas lights, but unlike the arc-light contingent, which was compelled by its light's brightness to develop outdoor systems, he focused indoors. Indoor gas-lighting systems were Edison's real competitors; he sought to create a DC incandescent system that would offer as much illumination (about sixteen-candle power) as gas lights, at a lower or equivalent price. He tackled the problem by first analyzing indoor gas lighting's costs. This was his single most important calculation, and would guide his attempt to produce an incandescent lighting system.

Edison decided to pursue incandescent lighting seriously in fall 1878. A public relations blitz accompanied that decision; Edison asserted in newspapers his priority in the field—in fact, he had done virtually nothing—and assured an attentive public that results soon would be forthcoming. Edison excelled at this type of campaign; it preempted other investors' claims, garnered him additional financial support, and began to accustom his market

A "Jumbo" dynamo, an electrical generator designed by Edison and his team helped to distribute electricity with increased efficiency.

to the anticipated new technology. Even as he puffed his venture, Edison computed that an economically feasible system would require high-resistance filament lamps and parallel wiring. The former would reduce copper wiring costs substantially, while the latter would ensure uninterrupted service. During late 1878 and 1879, Edison and his associates experimented with materials of various compositions and shapes to devise appropriate filaments, always removing gases occluded in filaments by continuing to evacuate bulbs during heating; Edison's team had found that filaments often contained oxides, the oxygen from which was liberated during the initial heating, causing the filaments to burn. They also investigated electrical generators and designed efficient, low-internal-resistance dynamos suitable for parallel lighting. Edison named these devices Jumbo generators after the great elephant brought to America by P.T. Barnum; Edison appreciated Barnum's adroit use of publicity.

THE FIRST POWER STATION

Edison's crew devoted themselves to developing the system's other components in 1880 and 1881. They devised safety fuses to prevent fires, and manufactured lighting fixtures, bulbs, and sockets for household use. Edison himself envisioned a feeder–main distribution network to cut copper wire costs by about 85 percent; rather than attach large copper mains directly to generators, thin feeder lines would carry current from dynamos to short sections of mains placed at points of dense electrical distribution. Pilot projects were established at Menlo Park [New Jersey] and London to demonstrate the system's feasibility and to work out bugs. By late 1881, Edison was ready to construct his first American commercial central station; he placed it at 257 Pearl Street, in the heart of New York City's financial community. Edison men laid underground conduits, and insulated the wires with hot asphaltum. They wired households and establishments, and installed meters based on electrolytic deposit of zinc to measure individual electric usage. Jumbo generators drove the DC system and were regulated individually by handwheels, which increased or decreased field resistance when turned to produce a relatively constant voltage. The Pearl Street station began operation on September 4, 1882, and Edison distributed electricity free for the remainder of the year to induce reluctant New Yorkers to tap into the system.

To Edison, Pearl Street was merely the first of what he assumed would be hundreds of stations located throughout America.

European Imperialism Reaches Its Peak

CHAPTER 3

THE SCRAMBLE FOR AFRICA

ROLAND OLIVER AND J.D. FAGE

In the following selection, historians Roland Oliver and J.D. Fage describe how, between 1870 and 1900, European powers raced to establish colonies in Africa. They argue that the main cause of the scramble for Africa, as it is generally known, was the emergence of two new colonial powers: Belgium under the aggressive and ambitious King Leopold II and the newly unified nation of Germany. Both sought to counter French and English claims to Africa while taking advantage of the continent's natural resources.

The scramble for Africa is perhaps the most dramatic example of Europe's rampant imperialist attitude in the late 1800s. As Oliver and Fage note, the European presence in Africa was small earlier in the century, meaning that by 1870 imperialists saw the continent as a blank slate, primed for European expansion. By 1900 only two African nations remained truly independent: Liberia, established by Americans to repatriate African slaves; and the ancient Christian kingdom of Ethiopia. The remainder of the continent had been carved up by the European powers.

Roland Oliver is professor of history at Cambridge University. J.D. Fage is professor of history at the University of Birmingham.

I n 1879, despite the steady increase in the power of the western European nations compared with that of other peoples in the world, only a small proportion of the African continent was under European rule. Algeria was French, but elsewhere in North Africa it was only in Egypt and in Tunis that there existed even the beginnings of European control. In West Africa, where

Excerpted from *A Short History of Africa* by Roland Oliver and J.D. Fage (Penguin Books, 1962, 6th ed., 1988). Copyright Roland Oliver and J.D. Fage, 1962, 1966, 1970, 1972, 1975, 1988. Reproduced by permission of Penguin Books Ltd.

Europeans had had commercial dealings with the coastal peoples for four centuries, it was only in French Senegal and on the British Gold Coast that there were colonial administrations ruling any considerable number of Africans. . . .

North of Moçambique [in East Africa], even the coast was still virtually untouched by European political power. British diplomatic influence was strong in Zanzibar. The French had occupied the Comoros and also had a foothold in Madagascar. On the mainland, however, it was only in the extreme north-east that any European flag had yet been planted. This was a consequence of the Suez Canal, the construction of which had led France to seek a counterpoise to the British coaling station at Aden by establishing a base on the inhospitable Somali coast at Obok. The only really deep penetration of Africa by European governments was in the extreme south, but here the position was complicated by the hostility between the British colonies on the coast and the Afrikaner communities in the interior.

Two decades later, however, at the beginning of the twentieth century, European governments were claiming sovereignty over all but six of some forty political units into which they had by then divided the continent—and of these six exceptions, four were more technical than real. This partition of Africa at the end of the nineteenth century was by no means a necessary consequence of the opening up of Africa by Europeans during the first three-quarters of the century. Very few indeed of the explorers of Africa had been sent by their governments to spy out the land for later conquest. It is probably safe to say that not a single missionary had ever imagined himself as serving in the vanguard of colonialism. In so far as there was an economic motive for partition of the kind suggested by Marxist writers, it was a motive which appealed to those European powers which had no colonies and little commercial influence in Africa, rather than to those whose influence was already established there. The partition of Africa was indeed essentially the result of the appearance on the African scene of one or two powers which had not previously shown any interest in the continent. It was this that upset the pre-existing balance of power and influence and precipitated a state of international hysteria in which all the powers rushed in to stake claims to political sovereignty and to bargain furiously with each other for recognition in this or that region.

THE KING OF BELGIUM SEEKS AN EMPIRE

The first of these new factors to enter the African scene was not strictly speaking a power. It was a European sovereign acting in

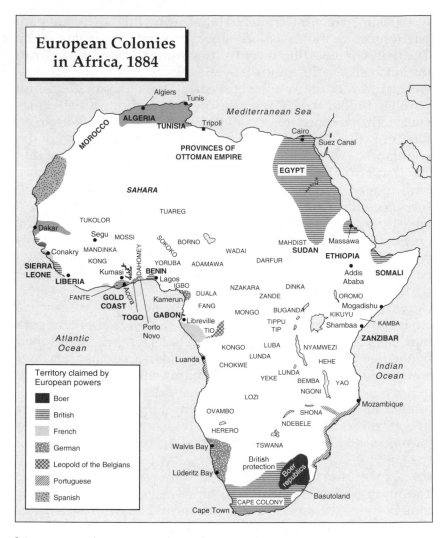

European Colonies in Africa, 1884

Algiers
Tunis
Mediterranean Sea
ALGERIA
TUNISIA
Tripoli
Cairo
Suez Canal
MOROCCO
PROVINCES OF
OTTOMAN EMPIRE
EGYPT
SAHARA
TUAREG
TUKOLOR
Dakar
Segu MOSSI
BORNO
MAHDIST Massawa
Conakry MANDINKA
WADAI
DARFUR SUDAN ETHIOPIA
SOKOTO
KONG
YORUBA ADAMAWA
SIERRA
LEONE
DAHOMEY
BENIN
Addis
Ababa SOMALI
Kumasi
LIBERIA
Lagos
IGBO
FANTE GOLD
COAST Kamerun DUALA NZAKARA DINKA
Accra
TOGO GABON
Libreville
FANG
ZANDE
MONGO BUGANDA OROMO Mogadishu
KIKUYU
Porto
Novo TIO TIPPU
TIP Shambaa KAMBA
*Atlantic
Ocean* Luanda KONGO LUBA NYAMWEZI ZANZIBAR
LUNDA
CHOKWE HEHE *Indian
Ocean*
YEKE LUNDA
BEMBA YAO
LOZI NGONI
Mozambique
OVAMBO SHONA
HERERO NDEBELE
Walvis Bay TSWANA
British
protection Boer
republics
Lüderitz Bay
CAPE COLONY Basutoland
Cape Town

Territory claimed by
European powers

- Boer
- British
- French
- German
- Leopold of the Belgians
- Portuguese
- Spanish

his personal capacity, though using his status as a sovereign to manipulate the threads of international diplomacy in pursuit of his private objective. King Leopold II of the Belgians was a man whose ambitions and capacities far outran the introverted preoccupations of the country he had been born to rule. His interest in founding an overseas empire had started in the 1850s and 1860s when as Duke of Brabant he had travelled in Egypt and had also scanned possible openings in places as remote as Formosa, Sarawak, Fiji, and the New Hebrides. Succeeding to the throne in 1865, he bent most of his great energies to the study of African exploration. Ten years later he was ready to act. His cover was the African International Association, created in 1876 to found a chain of commercial and scientific stations running across central Africa from Zanzibar to the Atlantic. The stations were to be garrisoned, and they were to serve as bases from which to attack the slave trade and to protect Christian missions. The first two expeditions of the Association entered East Africa from Zanzibar in 1878 and 1879, and attached themselves to mission stations of the White Fathers at Tabora and on Lake Tanganyika. From this moment, however, Leopold's interests switched increasingly to the west coast of Bantu Africa. Stanley, who in 1877 had completed his coast-to-coast journey by descending the Congo River, took service under King Leopold in 1879, and during the next five years established a practicable land and water transport system from the head of the Congo estuary to Stanley Falls, more than a thousand miles upstream, at the modern Stanleyville.

Leopold, meanwhile, was deftly preparing the way for international recognition of his rule over the whole area of the Congo basin. Although his real intention was to develop his colony on the basis of a close-fisted commercial monopoly, he was successful in persuading a majority of the European powers that it would be preferable to have the Congo basin as a free-trade area under his 'international' régime than to let it fall to any of their national rivals. The skill of King Leopold's diplomacy has been widely recognized. What has received less notice is the extent to which it sharpened the mutual suspicions of the European powers about their activities in Africa as a whole. Probably it was Leopold, more than any other single statesman, who created the 'atmosphere' of scramble.

THE GERMAN EMPIRE EXTENDS TO AFRICA

The next power to enter the African scene was Germany. Acting with stealth and swiftness in the eighteen months from the end of 1883 to the beginning of 1885, Germany made extensive annexations in four widely-separated parts of the continent—South-West Africa, Togoland, the Cameroons, and East Africa. It was this German action which was really to let loose the scramble on a scale bound to continue with ever-increasing intensity until the whole continent was partitioned. It is therefore the more remarkable that recent historical research has tended to show that Germany entered Africa, not primarily in order to satisfy a desire for empire there, but rather as part of a much wider design to deflect French hostility against her in Europe by fomenting rivalries in Africa and by creating a situation in which Germany would be the arbiter between French and British ambitions. . . .

Such then was the motivation for the scramble. To the three powers already engaged on the African coastline—Britain, France, and Portugal—there were now added two more, one of them a European sovereign in search of a personal empire, the other the strongest state in continental Europe, seeking to induce the most recent victim of its aggression to wear out its resentment in colonial adventure. In the circumstances, partition was bound to follow. . . .

As it happened, the first to secure international recognition of a large African empire was King Leopold. In 1884, after the British merchants engaged in the Congo trade had opposed their government's intention of recognizing Portuguese claims to the lower Congo region, Portugal changed tack and instead appealed to France and Germany for support. France, seeing a chance to embarrass Britain, agreed to Bismarck's suggestion of determining the Congo question by an international conference in Berlin. And even before this conference could meet, France (having made a deal with King Leopold by which she secured the reversion of his Congo empire in case its development became too much for his resources) had joined Germany and the United States in granting recognition to the 'Congo Free State'. When the conference met in December 1884, the other powers had no option but to follow suit.

DIVIDING AFRICA AT THE CONFERENCE TABLE

The Berlin Conference passed many high-sounding resolutions on the slave trade, on free trade, and on the need to prove effective occupation before fresh annexations were declared. In fact, however, the six months during which the conference was being prepared had seen the most flimsily-supported annexations in the whole partition, those of Germany herself. While the conference was actually sitting, Bismarck announced his government's protectorate over those parts of East Africa where Karl Peters and his associates had obtained dubious treaties from bemused and often bogus 'chiefs' in the course of a single expedition lasting a few weeks. It was now clear to all that a quick partition of the whole continent was inevitable, and the delegates went home from Berlin at the beginning of 1885 to consider where further claims for their own countries could most usefully be developed.

A Vietnamese Official Adjusts to French Rule

Duong Van Mai Elliot

After 1850 the French sought to acquire a global empire to balance that being assembled by the British. To counter British control of India as well as take advantage of the natural resources of the Mekong River region of Southeast Asia, the French colonized Asian territory they called French Indochina. It consisted of Laos, Cambodia, and the three kingdoms that today make up the nation of Vietnam: Tonkin, Annam, and Hue.

In the following selection from her family memoir, Duong Van Mai Elliot describes how her great-grandfather, an official in Hue, adapted to the French takeover of his country. Elliot notes that her great-grandfather maintained an important post and continued to live with dignity, but found working for the French a great blow to his pride.

Duong Van Mai Elliot was born in Vietnam and, after an American education, lived there during the Vietnam War, where she worked interviewing prisoners of war.

After sweeping royal authority away in Tonkin, the French proceeded to emasculate the court in Hue. The emperor became only a figurehead. The royal decrees might bear his name, but the French were behind the decisions. In the case of my great-grandfather, they were the ones that approved his promotion to governor general, and they were the ones that told the emperor to grant him the title of Baron of Khanh Van. The court was powerless. The French now held the purse strings. Instead of controlling the country's treasury, the emperor received a monthly stipend for himself and his family. After pushing the anemic court to the side, the French set out to create a new and more modern government apparatus, with agencies like customs and management of state monopolies (of opium, salt, and alcohol), public works, agriculture, commerce, postal service, and communication. Vietnam was no longer a nation, but three distinct parts: the colony of Cochinchina and the protectorates of Annam and Tonkin. Then all three were merged with Laos and Cambodia to form the Union of Indochina. The French governor general, headquartered in Saigon, became the ruler of this forced union.

SADDENED BY THE FRENCH TAKEOVER

Although my great-grandfather's career was not immediately damaged by the French annexation, he viewed this turning point in his country's history as one of the saddest periods in his life. In the autobiographical poem he wrote for his family two years before his death to review his experiences and teach his descendants how to live by the same traditional values he had obeyed, he compared the situation in 1897 when the French swept away royal authority to the end of a chess game—with the Hue court checkmated—and to a withering flower about to die. For a man who admired his country's achievement and tradition, the annexation was a blow to national pride. He also took it as a blow to his own pride. In the same poem, he expressed his feeling of impotence in stopping the decline and chided himself for his failure.

But as much as he resented this foreign yoke, he had to suppress his hostility and maintain a facade of civility toward the French, with whom he corresponded in the traditional flowery language of the scholar and official, full of exaggerated courtesy ("You are like a star in the firmament") and humble references to himself ("I am but dust and ashes"). In truth, he did not dislike all the colonial officials he met, and seemed to have been friendly with some of them, such as the *résident* [head French official] in Hung Yen Province, whom he asked to look after his oldest son before he left for his post in central Vietnam. For their part, the French also had an ambivalent attitude toward him. Most of the colonial officials he dealt with recognized his intelligence and leadership and were anxious not to alienate him. But because of the continuing opposition among many mandarins, they never completely relaxed their vigilance over him.

As my great-grandfather must have known when he decided to "engage" himself, this relationship with the French authorities—however ambivalent and reluctant—could tarnish his reputation not only during this lifetime, but also in the verdict of history. Through the good he accomplished, he managed to retain the respect of his contemporaries in a very difficult situation and at a time when the public was quick to condemn mandarins who collaborated with the French. My family still retains the text of an anonymous poem that was posted to the gate of Hoang Cao Khai, the last viceroy of Tonkin, on the occasion of one of his birthdays. Each year, on the viceroy's birthday, all the high-ranking mandarins had to troop to his residence to pay their respects. The poem's anonymous author took this opportunity to express his contempt and hatred for several of the officials present at the celebration, condemning them for their venality and cruelty, but praising Duong Lam [the author's great grandfather] and his brother Duong Khue for their filial piety and detachment from the unscrupulous activities of their colleagues. It was a tacit recognition that they had not abused their power.

As for the verdict of history, it remains critical. Although collaboration would become widespread over the eighty years of colonial rule, leaving few of the elite untouched, modern historians in general continue to condemn high-ranking mandarins of Duong Lam's generation for their association with the French. In my great-grandfather's case, there was an undercurrent of criticism that sometimes erupted into print after his death. He was usually attacked not for anything specific, but for pursuing power and prestige when he should have withdrawn from service.

CONTINUING TO LIVE A FULL LIFE

My great-grandfather did not let his concern over his country's state of affairs or his anxiety over whether or not to serve keep him from living fully. He was a vigorous man who knew how to appreciate the good things in life. My parents remembered him as an intimidating figure and yet one with a laugh "so resonant it could be heard in the street," who enjoyed food, wine, and song, but in moderation, as dictated by Confucian rules of behavior. He had a good sense of humor and could laugh at himself. He was not demanding in his tastes and could easily adjust to whatever circumstances in which he found himself: He was just as content eating a humble meal as one full of delicacies, dressing in the finest brocades or in rough cotton. Of course, like all traditional scholars, my great-grandfather loved philosophy and literature, especially poetry, which he considered the most refined and accomplished of the art forms. Like other scholars, he enjoyed reciting and composing poems in the company of friends. On these occasions, wine would flow. His and his guests would drink cup after cup, to put themselves in a better mood to savor the beauty of the verses. These and other poems he wrote were mostly for the enjoyment of himself and his friends or family.

My great-grandfather also appreciated chess and a good card game, mostly for the social aspects. He also loved music and the company of female singers, whom he frequently hired to perform for him and his friends, or visited in their quarters. In the red-light district, singers would ply their clients with food and wine and entertain them with songs. But my great-grandfather's interest in the singers was connected to his love of poetry, since the songs were poems chanted to the accompaniment of musical instruments. He himself wrote several compositions for the singers, some of which he dedicated to those whose talent he appreciated the most, or those with whom he had carried on short liaisons.

Mastery of Radio Waves

Arthur C. Clarke

Nineteenth-century inventions revolutionized mass communications. The telegraph, invented in the 1840s, allowed messages to be sent via cables that, by the first years of the twentieth century, stretched around the globe. The telegraph was followed by the telephone in 1876. Telephone use grew quickly, and by 1900 more than a million miles of telephone cable had been laid in the United States.

An important next step is described by Arthur C. Clarke in the following selection. This was the invention of the radio, the "wireless telegraph." Clarke notes that the first to successfully transmit radio waves was the Italian engineer Guglielmo Marconi in 1894. Within only seven years Marconi was able to send wireless messages across the Atlantic Ocean. As Clarke points out, subsequent inventors found ways to both improve and magnify radio waves. By 1910 the electronic age was under way.

Arthur C. Clarke, the author of dozens of books, is a highly respected writer on scientific subjects as well as of science fiction.

I t is seldom that a single man dominates an important and rapidly expanding field of technology, but for thirty years [Guglielmo] Marconi was the Colossus of radio. He was scarcely out of his teens when he succeeded in sending radio waves for a distance of a mile near Bologna, Italy, and two years later—in 1896—he moved to England, where many of his most famous experiments were carried out, frequently in connection with the British Post Office.

Very early in the development of the art, it was discovered that radio transmitting and receiving equipment could be tuned, so that one could choose the station one wished to listen to, and ignore all others. We take this so much for granted that it is hard to realize that someone had to discover it; the credit is due to Sir Oliver Lodge, who first demonstrated the principle in 1897.

As the twentieth century dawned, radio (or wireless, as most people then called it) rapidly extended its range, and in 1901 it leaped the Atlantic. Flying a receiving antenna

Guglielmo Marconi

from a kite in Newfoundland, Marconi was able to pick up Morse signals transmitted from Poldhu, Cornwall [in southwestern England].

Here was a first-class mystery. *If* radio waves behaved like light, there was no way in which they could bend round the curve of the earth. A searchlight in Cornwall, no matter how powerful it was, could not be seen more than a few score miles out in the Atlantic; after that distance its rays would have arrowed on out into space, high above the falling curve of the world.

In 1902 [mathematician] Oliver Heaviside proposed an explanation which seemed almost as farfetched as the facts. They suggested that, at a very great altitude in the atmosphere, there was a reflecting layer which turned radio waves back to earth, so that they did not escape into space. As it seemed most unlikely that nature should be so considerate to the communications industry, and it was also hard to see what could create a layer with such peculiar properties, scientists were slow in accepting this explanation. Not until 1924—only two months before Heaviside's death—did [British scientists] Edward Appleton and Barnett prove conclusively that the upper atmosphere contained not only one reflecting layer but at least two. Today we have flown hundreds of rockets through the ionosphere, as it is now called, and soon we will be traveling through it ourselves.

Inventing the Electronic Age

The early radio workers had been hampered by two serious deficiencies in their equipment: their methods of detecting the waves were very insensitive and cumbersome, and they had no way of amplifying the signals when they had been receiving. Radio, in fact, was still in the pre–crystal-set stage.

The first major breakthrough came in 1904 when [bacteriologist John Ambrose] Fleming invented the diode valve, the primitive ancestor of all the billions of electron tubes in the world today. The name "valve" was accurate enough; the diode allowed signals to pass in one direction, but not in the other. It turned the rapidly-varying radio waves into audible signals—but it could not amplify them.

That essential step came in 1907, with [inventor Lee] De Forest's invention of the triode. By feeding the faint impulses to a wire-mesh grid strategically placed inside Fleming's diode, De Forest made the overwhelmingly important discovery that it was possible to amplify signals to an almost unlimited extent. The triode ushered in the electronic age, in whose first dawn we are now living, and was therefore one of the truly epoch-making inventions of history.

In the field of communications, where it received its first use, the triode and its more complex successors gave radio the basic tool needed for its swift development. Once the means for amplifying faint and rapidly-varying electric currents had been discovered, armies of ingenious engineers, with Marconi well in the forefront, worked out the rest of the radio technology and built up the most swiftly-expanding industry the world has ever seen.

THE AUTOMOBILE GROWS POPULAR

EUGEN WEBER

The technological achievements of the late nineteenth century built on each other, as inventors learned from their colleagues around the world and moved easily from one field of innovation to related fields. The same was true for those who appreciated new gadgets and devices, as Eugen Weber points out in the following passage. The first to drive automobiles in France were wealthy men and women who had embraced the bicycle, itself a recent invention. Nonetheless, as Weber goes on to assert, automobiles quickly grew in popularity thanks to France's system of roads, the many advantages cars seemed to offer, and the fact that cars clearly represented the innovative, energetic spirit of the age.

The first successful internal combustion engine was invented by the German Karl Benz in 1885. Soon afterward Gottlieb Daimler built a four-wheeled vehicle around it and obtained a license to produce his new machine in France. The door had been opened and soon other innovators, including such still familiar names as Peugeot and Ford, found ways to make automobiles better and cheaper.

Eugen Weber is professor of history at the University of California, Los Angeles.

L ike bicycles, horseless carriages operated by steam, compressed air, electricity, or a variety of fuels had been around since the eighteenth century. In 1885, however, Karl Benz, a German, invented a petrol engine that worked. In 1891 Armand Peugeot, who had turned the family hardware manufacture from farm implements, umbrella spokes, and corset stays to bicycles, built a small car in which he traveled from Montbéliard in eastern France to Paris, then followed a bicycle race to Brest and back at an average speed of ten miles per hour, before returning home—2,500 kilometers later—without a problem. By 1895 Peugeot had sold two hundred vehicles—two-fifths of those then being driven on the roads of France. The cars built by Peugeot, Panhard, Levassor, and others were for the rich alone. Custom-made, they might cost 40 to 50,000 francs to build, and several thousand francs a year to run. One owner paid 1,500 francs a year (a workingman's total income) simply for new tires.

The spirit and enterprise which built and raced motor cars—and airplanes not long afterward—were kin to those which launched the velocipede. Cycling enthusiasts bought and drove the first automobiles. As in the United States, where the Wright brothers and Glenn Curtis started out building bikes, many cycle manufacturers, like Adolphe Clément, turned to building cars, then airships and airplane engines. Cycle racers like the Farman brothers built and raced motor cycles and motor cars before they turned to aviation. Hélène Dutrieu, winner of the world cycling title in 1898, would go on to get her pilot's license and establish a whole series of flying records before World War I broke out. Nor was this surprising. The components of cars, cycles, and planes of those early days were often the same. So was the inspiration of those who made them and who made them run: love of danger and novelty, of speed and adventure.

AN ADVENTURE SEEKER

The figure of Albert, Marquis de Dion (1851–1946), though generally remembered by the courtesy title of Count that he carried until his father's death, is typical of early automobile enthusiasts. In the 1880s Dion entered into an association with a mechanic, Georges Bouton, to build steam boilers, steam tricycles, and steam carriages, some of which he then drove to victory in a number of road races. In 1895 he built a petrol-driven tricycle, then a real automobile, and began to experiment with cheaper models. In this he was overtaken by Louis Renault's more innovative designs, which combined lightness with greater horsepower (Dion did not believe in multicylinder engines). Dion also found time to found the Automobile Club de France (1895) and—earnest of his adventurous nature—the Aéro Club de France (1898). The pugnacity that made him risk family disapproval and public scorn for his mechanical extravagances was reflected in his politics. An ardent anti-Dreyfusard, he was one of the group arrested at the Auteuil races in June 1899 for attacking President

Loubet. This reflected the political coloring of the Automobile Club, with its fine palace on the place de la Concorde and its membership of wealthy, titled, and reactionary *automobilistes;* and the club itself was briefly closed down after this escapade as a den of conspirators against the Republic. Dion, however, whose only idea of flight was to charge forward, ran for election as a Nationalist in the Loire-Inférieure and was elected departmental councillor, then deputy, and eventually senator of this solidly Monarchist and Catholic region. Nor did that lessen his interest in building and racing autos; in 1907 he joined the newspaper *Le Matin* in organizing a spectacular International Rally from Paris to Peking.

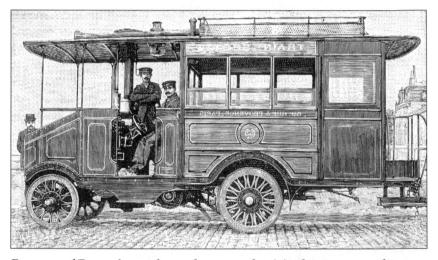

Because of France's ample roadways and spirited auto races, the popularity of automobiles soared among wealthy citizens.

Racing was dangerous but it sold cars as it had sold bicycles before them. Competition between manufacturers—fin de siècle [end of the century] France had more than any other country—made their publicity crucial. Renault, like other pioneers, raced his own cars to bring them to the public eye and prove that small, light vehicles performed as well as or better than larger ones. In 1901 he won first place in his category in the Paris-Berlin race and had to double the capacity of his works at Billancourt, near Paris. In 1902 his brother Marcel came out first overall in the Paris–Vienna run, at an average speed of 39 mph—faster than the fastest train in Europe, the Arlberg Express. Marcel would kill himself the following year, missing a dangerous curve in a cloud of dust while trying to overtake a competitor during the Paris–Madrid race; after this the government prohibited road races as being too murderous, allowing only closed-circuit ones as at Le Mans. But the Billancourt firm never looked back.

Although France had the best roads in Europe, their quality was relative. Automobiles proceeded in a cloud of dust that blinded and choked other drivers or users of the road—and often, as with Marcel Renault, the conductor himself. Rudyard Kipling remembered "the soft roads that went to pieces under the tires and revenged themselves by breaking the strongest springs"—as well as the tires. He recalled that chauffeurs and passengers were not only muffled and goggled against the dust and wind, but equipped with a long-lashed whip to ward off dogs. Despite such drawbacks, the automobile forged ahead, in part because it promised to reduce the noise, congestion, and pollution of city streets in process of being increasingly overwhelmed by traffic. True, cars smelled bad and made a lot of noise, but they would displace the horse which also smelled and cost a lot of money. Above all, they represented progress and "the triumph of regenerating sports which would forge a strong race."

LIFE SPEEDS UP

They were certainly forging an increasingly speedy one. Taxicabs were replacing horsecabs, even in provincial towns; bandits and police adopted the new means of locomotion; municipalities regulated their use. In 1909 Deauville counted 2,218 cars (and 896 horse-drawn carriages) at its annual races; by 1912, 3,613 cars (no carriages) were encountering parking problems there. The hippodrome had built a special garage for bicycles in 1893. Now, the eight hundred slots of the new *vestiaire de voitures* [parking garage] did not suffice. Courts of law began to fine imprudent drivers and to regulate their speed. But the intelligence that more French were dying from bicycle and automobile accidents than died from drinking was greeted calmly by those aware that bolting horses had frequently caused accidents and injuries. In December 1901 the Fourth Salon of Bicycles and Autos, inaugurated by the President of the Republic, welcomed 40,000 visitors a day to look over the 693 different automobiles and the 645 bicycle models on show. A ten-horsepower car still cost 8,000 francs, but Louis Renault's new chassis sold for 1,500 francs, and Dion was about to bring out his suggestively named "La Populaire." [The journal] *L'Illustration* opined that automobiles could actually prove useful: more than toys for millionaires, they represented the beginning of profound economic changes that would affect everyone.

THE BALLAD OF EAST AND WEST

RUDYARD KIPLING

The following poem is by Rudyard Kipling, who was born in British India and worked there as a journalist for a number of years in the 1880s. Kipling, awarded the Nobel Prize in literature in 1907, is remembered for such stories as *The Jungle Book* and *Kim* as well as his poetry. His work is considered important for both its depictions of British India and its expression of the imperialist sentiments of his era.

The poem's setting is the borderland between British India and Afghanistan, a site of constant conflict because of the numerous lawless tribes who lived there who only occasionally recognized British authority. Kipling's main characters are Kamal, a border chieftain, and an officer in the Queen's Own Corps of Guides, an elite British army unit that patrolled the border. The main theme is the honor of warriors (as well as, perhaps, the ultimate superiority of the British), as Kamal recognizes the British officer as a great soldier and sends his son to join the guides as a "Ressaldar," or cavalry officer.

THE BALLAD OF EAST AND WEST
1889

O
H, EAST *is East, and West is West, and never the twain shall*
meet,
Till Earth and Sky stand presently at God's great Judgment Seat;
But there is neither East nor West, Border, nor Breed, nor Birth,
When two strong men stand face to face, though they come from the
ends of the earth!

Reprinted from "The Ballad of East and West," by Rudyard Kipling, 1889.

Kamal is out with twenty men to raise the Border-side,
And he has lifted the Colonel's mare that is the Colonel's pride.
He has lifted her out of the stable-door between the dawn and the day,
And turned the calkins upon her feet, and ridden her far away.
Then up and spoke the Colonel's son that led a troop of the Guides:
"Is there never a man of all my men can say where Kamal hides?"
Then up and spoke Mohammed Khan, the son of the Ressaldar:
"If ye know the track of the morning-mist, ye know where his pickets are.
"At dust he harries the Abazai—at dawn he is into Bonair,
"But he must go by Fort Bukloh to his own place to fare.
"So if ye gallop to Fort Bukloh as fast as a bird can fly,
"By the favour of God ye may cut him off ere he win to the Tongue of Jagai.
"But if he be past the Tongue of Jagai, right swiftly turn ye then,
"For the length and the breadth of that grisly plain is sown with Kamal's men.
"There is rock to the left, and rock to the right, and low lean thorn between,
"And ye may hear a breech-bolt snick where never a man is seen."
The Colonel's son has taken horse, and a raw rough dun was he,
With the mouth of a bell and the heart of Hell and the head of a gallows-tree.
The Colonel's son to the Fort has won, they bid him stay to eat
Who rides at the tail of a Border thief, he sits not long at his meat.
He's up and away from Fort Bukloh as fast as he can fly,
Till he was aware of his father's mare in the gut of the Tongue of Jagai,
Till he was aware of his father's mare with Kamal upon her back,
And when he could spy the white of her eye, he made the pistol crack.
He has fired once, he has fired twice, but the whistling ball went wide.
"Ye shoot like a soldier," Kamal said. "Show now if ye can ride!"
It's up and over the Tongue of Jagai, as blown dust-devils go,
The dun he fled like a stag of ten, but the mare like a barren doe.
The dun he leaned against the bit and slugged his head above,
But the red mare played with the snaffle-bars, as a maiden plays with a glove.
There was rock to the left and rock to the right, and low lean thorn between,
And thrice he heard a breech-bolt snick tho' never a man was seen.

They have ridden the low moon out of the sky, their hoofs drum
   up the dawn,
The dun he went like a wounded bull, but the mare like a new-
   roused fawn.
The dun he fell at a water-course—in a woeful heap fell he,
And Kamal has turned the red mare back, and pulled the rider
   free.
He has knocked the pistol out of his hand—small room was there
   to strive,
"'Twas only by favour of mine," quoth he, "ye rode so long alive:
"There was not a rock for twenty mile, there was not a clump of
   tree,
"But covered a man of my own men with his rifle cocked on his
   knee.
"If I had raised my bridle-hand, as I have held it low,
"The little jackals that flee so fast were feasting all in a row.
"If I had bowed my head on my breast, as I have held it high,
"The kite that whistles above us now were gorged till she could
   not fly."
Lightly answered the Colonel's son: "Do good to bird and beast,
"But count who come for the broken meats before thou makest a
   feast.
"If there should follow a thousand swords to carry my bones
   away,
"Belike the price of a jackal's meal were more than a thief could
   pay.
"They will feed their horse on the standing crop, their men on
   the garnered grain.
"The thatch of the byres will serve their fires when all the cattle
   are slain.
"But if thou thinkest the price be fair,—thy brethren wait to sup,
"The hound is kin to the jackal-spawn,—howl, dog, and call
   them up!
"And if thou thinkest the price be high, in steer and gear and
   stack,
"Give me my father's mare again, and I'll fight my own way
   back!"
Kamal has gripped him by the hand and set him upon his feet.
"No talk shall be of dogs," said he, "when wolf and grey wolf
   meet.
"May I eat dirt if thou hast hurt of me in deed or breath;
"What dam of lances brought thee forth to jest at the dawn with
   Death?"
Lightly answered the Colonel's son: "I hold by the blood of my
   clan:

"Take up the mare for my father's gift—by God, she has carried
a man!"
The red mare ran to the Colonel's son, and nuzzled against his
breast;
"We be two strong men," said Kamal then, "but she loveth the
younger best.
"So she shall go with a lifter's dower, my turquoise-studded rein,
"My 'broidered saddle and saddle-cloth, and silver stirrups twain."
The Colonel's son a pistol drew, and held it muzzle-end,
"Ye have taken the one from a foe," said he. "Will ye take the
mate from a friend?"
"A gift for a gift," said Kamal straight; "a limb for the risk of a
limb.
"Thy father has sent his son to me, I'll send my son to him!"
With that he whistled his only son, that dropped from a mountain-
crest—
He trod the ling like a buck in spring, and he looked like a lance
in rest.
"Now here is thy master," Kamal said, "who leads a troop of the
Guides,
"And thou must ride at his left side as shield on shoulder rides.
"Till Death or I cut loose the tie, at camp and board and bed,
"Thy life is his—thy fate it is to guard him with thy head.
"So, thou must eat the White Queen's meat, and all her foes are
thine,
"And thou must harry thy father's hold for the peace of the
Border-line.
"And thou must make a trooper tough and hack thy way to
power—
"Belike they will raise thee to Ressaldar when I am hanged in Pe-
shawur!"

They have looked each other between the eyes, and there they
found no fault.
They have taken the Oath of the Brother-in-Blood on leavened
bread and salt:
They have taken the Oath of the Brother-in-Blood on fire and
fresh-cut sod,
On the hilt and the haft of the Khyber knife, and the Wondrous
Names of God.
The Colonel's son he rides the mare and Kamal's boy the dun,
And two have come back to Fort Bukloh where there went forth
but one.
And when they drew to the Quarter-Guard, full twenty swords
flew clear—

There was not a man but carried his feud with the blood of the
  mountaineer.
"Ha' done! ha' done!" said the Colonel's son. "Put up the steel at
  your sides!
"Last night ye had struck at a Border thief—to-night 'tis a man
  of the Guides!"

Oh, East is East, and West is West, and never the twain shall meet,
Till Earth and Sky stand presently at God's great Judgment Seat;
But there is neither East nor West, Border, nor Breed, nor Birth,
When two strong men stand face to face, though they come from the
  ends of the earth!

GREAT BRITAIN CELEBRATES QUEEN AND EMPIRE

JAN MORRIS

In 1897, Britain's Queen Victoria celebrated her sixtieth year on the throne. During her reign Britain had become the greatest imperial power on earth, claiming dominion over one-fourth of the world's land and people. In the following selection, Jan Morris asserts that the celebration of Victoria's Diamond Jubilee was also an occasion to celebrate the British Empire. The parades before the queen featured soldiers and diplomats from all over the world, as well as a huge variety of goods and curios.

Morris claims that the British felt they had much to celebrate in 1897. They believed, she asserts, in the historical greatness of Britain, which carried with it a duty to bring the benefits of British civilization to colonized peoples. Moreover, the empire supplied Britain with natural resources, markets, and strategic advantages that allowed it to remain wealthy and powerful in the face of rivals such as Germany and the United States.

Jan Morris is a prolific historian and travel writer whose books include *The Pax Britannica Trilogy*, *The Spectacle of Empire*, *Hong Kong*, and *Destinations*.

Queen Victoria of England went home happy on her Diamond Jubilee day, June 22, 1897. History had humoured her, as she deserved. The sun had shone all day—'Queen's weather', the English called it—and there was nothing artificial to the affection her people had shown during her hours of celebration. She had passed in procession through London intermittently weeping for pleasure, and studded her diary that evening with joyous adjectives: indescribable, truly marvellous, deeply touching.

It was more than a personal happiness, more even than a national rejoicing, for the British had chosen to commemorate the Diamond Jubilee as a festival of Empire. They were in possession that day of the largest Empire ever known to history, and since a large part of it had been acquired during the sixty years of Victoria's reign, it seemed proper to honour the one with the other. It would mark this moment of British history, as an Imperial moment, a Roman moment. It would proclaim to the world, flamboyantly, that England was far more than England: that beneath the Queen's dominion lay a quarter of the earth's land surface, and nearly a quarter of its people—literally, as Christopher North the poet had long before declared it, an Empire on which the sun never set.

So the day had been a proud, gaudy, sentimental, glorious day. This was *fin de siècle* [the end of the century]. The public taste was for things theatrical. Statesmen and generals were actors themselves, and here was the brassiest show on earth. Through the grey and venerable streets of the capital—'the greatest city since the ruin of Thebes'—there had passed in parade a spectacle of Empire. There were Rajput princes [from India] and Dyak headhunters [from Borneo], there were strapping troopers from Australia. Cypriots wore fezzes, Chinese wore conical straw hats. English gentlemen rode by, with virile moustaches and steel-blue eyes, and Indian lancers jangled past in resplendent crimson jerkins.

Here was Lord Roberts of Kandahar, on the grey Arab that had taken him from Kabul to Kandahar in his epic march of 1880. Here was Lord Worseley of Cairo and Wolseley, hero of Red River, Ashanti and Tel-el-Kebir. Loyal slogans fluttered through the streets—'One Race, One Queen'—'The Queen of Earthly Queens'—'God Bless Her Gracious Majesty!' Patriotic songs resounded. Outside St Paul's Cathedral, where the Prince of Wales received the Queen in her barouche, a service of thanksgiving was held, with archbishops officiating and an Empire in attendance.

That morning the Queen had telegraphed a jubilee message to all her subjects—to Africa and to Asia, to the cities of the Canadian West and the townships of New Zealand, to Gibraltar and Jamaica, to Lucknow and Rangoon, to sweltering primitives of the rainforests as to svelte merchant princes of the milder tropics. The occasion was grand. The audience was colossal. The symbolism was deliberate. The Queen's message, however, was simple. 'From my heart I thank my beloved people', she said. 'May God bless them.'

A Diverse Empire

'My people'. If to the Queen herself all the myriad peoples of the Empire really did seem one, to the outsider their unity seemed less than apparent. Part of the purpose of the jubilee jamboree was to give the Empire a new sense of cohesion: but it was like wishing reason upon the ocean, so enormous was the span of that association, and so unimaginable its contrasts and contradictions. Some of its constituents were complete modern nations, the self-governing white colonies in Australia, Canada, New Zealand and South Africa. Some were Crown Colonies governed, in one degree or another, direct from London. Some were protectorates so isolated and naive that the very idea of Empire was inconceivable to most of their inhabitants. At one extreme was India, a civilization in itself. at the other was Ascension, a mere speck in the South Atlantic, uninhabited by any kind of vertebrate until the British arrived. Every faith was represented in the British Empire, every colour of skin, every philosophy, almost every branch of human history. [Prime Minister] Disraeli had called it the most peculiar of all Empires, and so it was, for it was a gigantic jumble of origins, influences, attitudes and intentions.

The inhabitants of Tristan da Cunha (for example) had no government at all, and no written laws either. In India 1,000 British civil servants, protected by 70,000 British soldiers, ruled 300 million people in a sub-continent the size of Europe. In Cairo the residence of the British Agent and Consul-General was known to Egyptians as *Beit-al-Lurd*—House of the Lord. On Norfolk Island in the South Pacific citizens saluted each other with their traditional greeting 'Whataway you!' On Pitcairn the descendants of the Bounty mutineers were governed by their own President of Council.

In Mauritius that year crops were threatened by the plant pest *Cordia macrostachya*, brought there in 1890 from British Guiana. In Zanzibar the entire economy depended upon the cultivation of cloves, taken there in 1770 from Mauritius. Scottish gorse thrived on St Helena, Irish donkeys in South Africa, English stoats, hedgehogs, rooks and mice in New Zealand. The descendants of Canadian convicts, transported to Australia, still lived in Sydney. Mr Dadabhai Naoroji was Member of Parliament for Finsbury. In Aden the Parsees had their Tower of Silence, in Cape Town the Malays had their mosque, in Calcutta race-horses were habitually called Walers because they came, with their jockeys, from New South Wales. The bubonic plague had recently been introduced to India, by rats on board a ship from Hong Kong.

When Major Allan Wilson and thirty-two of his men were trapped on a river-bank by Matabele tribesmen in Rhodesia in

1893, they sang 'God Save the Queen' as they mustered back to back to defend themselves. When the gunboat HMS *Wasp* approached Tory Island off western Ireland to collect rates in 1897, the islanders revolved maledictive stones, and pronounced curses upon the vessel. When the Bishop of Gibraltar was received in audience by the Pope, the Pontiff remarked: 'I gather I am within your Lordship's diocese.'

If there was one characteristic diffused throughout this bewildering gallimaufry, it was an almost feverish enthusiasm. The mood of Empire in 1897 was *bravura*—'an attempt', as the painter Constable once defined it, at something beyond the truth. The British Empire was a heady outlet for the imagination of a people still in its prime. Its subjects were of all races: its activists were nearly all British. Through the gate of Empire Britons could escape from their cramped and rainy islands into places of grander scale and more vivid excitement, and since the Queen's accession at least 3 million had gone. By 1897 they were everywhere. There were Britons that year commanding the private armies of the Sultan of Sarawak, organizing the schedules of the mountain railway to Darjeeling, accepting the pleas of runaway slaves in Muscat, charting the China Sea, commanding the Mounties' post on the Chinook Pass in the Yukon, governing the Zulus and the Wa, invading the Sudan, laying telegraph wires across the Australian outback, editing the *Times of India*, prospecting for gold in the valley of the Limpopo, patrolling the Caribbean and investigating the legal system of the Sikhs—all within the framework of Empire, and under the aegis of the crown.

All this the Diamond Jubilee reflected. It was truly the Empire in little, as its organizers intended: a grand and somewhat vulgar spectacle, reflecting a tremendous and not always delicate adventure, and perfectly expressing the conviction of Cecil Rhodes, the imperial financier, that to be born British was to win first prize in the lottery of life.

THE BRITISH IMPERIAL TRADITION

The origins of the British Empire, like the form of it, were random. There had been British possessions overseas since the days of the Normans [in the eleventh century], who brought with them title to the Channel Islands and parts of France, and who presently seized Ireland too. Since then the imperial estate had fitfully grown. Sometimes possessions had been lost—the thirteen colonies of America, for instance, or the ancient possessions of the French mainland. Often they had been swapped, or voluntarily surrendered, or declined. Tangier, Sicily, Heligoland, Java, the Ionians, Minorca had all been British at one time or another. Costa Rica had applied unsuccessfully for a British protectorate, and Hawaii was British for five months in the 1840s. During Victoria's reign the expansion of the Empire had been more consistent. 'Acquired in a fit of absence of mind', the historian J.R. Seeley had said of it in a famous phrase, but in fact its piecemeal development had been conscious enough. Each step had its own logic: it was the whole resultant edifice that had an absent air.

Essentially most possessions were acquired for profit—for raw materials, for promising markets, for investment, or to deny commercial rivals undue advantages. As free traders the British had half-convinced themselves of a duty to keep protectionists out of undeveloped markets, and they were proud of the fact that when they acquired a new territory, its trade was open to all comers. Economics, though, must be sustained by strategy, and so the Empire generated its own extension. To protect ports, hinterlands must be acquired. To protect trade routes, bases were needed. One valley led to the next, each river to its headwaters, every sea to the other shore.

An Unquestioned Faith in Progress

To these material, if often misty impulses were added urges of a higher kind. At least since the start of the nineteenth century the British Empire had regarded itself as an improvement society, dedicated to the elevation of mankind. Raised to the summit of the world by their own systems, the British believed in progress as an absolute, and thought they held its keys. AUSPICIUM MELIORIS AEVI was the motto of the imperial order of chivalry, The Most Distinguished Order of St Michael and St George—'A Pledge of Better Times'. The British way was the true way, free trade to monarchy, and it was the privilege of Britons to propagate it across the world. Through the agency of Empire the slave trade had been abolished, and on the vehicle of Empire many a Christian mission had journeyed to its labours.

The desire to do good was a true energy of Empire, and with it went a genuine sense of duty—Christian duty, for though this was an Empire of multitudinous beliefs, its masters were overwhelmingly Church of England. Sometimes, especially in the middle of the nineteenth century, their duty was powerfully Old Testament in style, soldiers stormed about with Bibles in their hands, administrators sat like bearded prophets at their desks. By the 1890s it was more subdued, but still devoted to the principle that the British were some sort of Chosen People, touched on the shoulder by the Great Being, and commissioned to do His will in the world.

And of course, as in all great historical movements, the fundamental purpose was not a purpose at all, but simply an instinct. The British had reached an apogee. Rich, vigorous, inventive, more than 40 million strong, they had simply spilled out of their islands, impelled by forces beyond their own analysis. In this sense at least they were truly chosen. Destiny, an abstraction the imperialist poets loved to invoke, really had made of them a special kind of nation, and had distributed their ideas, their language, their ships and their persons uniquely across the world.

A EUROPEAN JEW EXPRESSES HIS HOPES FOR A JEWISH HOMELAND

THEODOR HERZL

By 1897 an Austrian journalist, Theodor Herzl, had become convinced that Europe's Jews would forever face anti-Semitism in Europe. Herzl started a movement known as Zionism, which sought to establish a Jewish homeland in Palestine, then part of the Turkish Ottoman Empire. Zionists made speeches, published articles, and raised funds in hopes of establishing communities of Jewish settlers in Palestine. Their efforts led to the modern State of Israel, established after the Holocaust of World War II.

The following document is a report by Herzl, published in the German newspaper *Die Welt* on November 18, 1898, of a visit he made to Palestine to solicit the approval of the Turkish sultan as well as the German emperor, whom Herzl saw as a potential ally. Herzl expresses his admiration for the hard work of Jewish settlers as well as his faith that a Palestine settled by Jews would be an asset to Turkey.

We did not go to Palestine as tourists or as explorers but with a definite political purpose. After our aim had been achieved, we immediately started on our trip home. Yet even as guests for a short time we were able to make some observations and get an idea of conditions. In many respects things look sad, but a magnificent sky smiles over the desolate, neglected places, and where human hands have been allowed to be active, an inexhaustible nature has cheerfully helped them to bring forth, as if by magic [and with the greatest speed], a profusion of products. The results achieved by our settlers, particularly those who are standing on their own two feet, are nothing short of amazing. One can still see the surrounding rocky, parched area which one such stalwart fellow entered a few years ago—but he has coaxed from that soil an orange grove or a lush vineyard.

Among these pioneer acquirers of land who are conquering the soil as at the beginning of time, the settler Brozie at Motzah near Jerusalem attracted my particular attention. He started out as a simple day laborer in the Rehovot settlement. One day he gathered up the meager funds which he had saved by starving himself and went out to that rocky mountain slope. Because he gave proof of his diligence, a settlement society in Cologne supported him with loans. Two years ago he had his first vintage; the yield was five hundred francs. The following year his vintage brought him three times that amount, and because his vines are getting better all the time, he is looking forward to a further rapid increase in his yield. His well-kept vineyard is still surrounded by a desert, but industrious people could turn that desert, too, into a garden.

The number of such examples is as great as the number of settlers in Palestine. These are capable, sober people with hard fists, and their eyes shine with enthusiasm for the land.

The Jewish farmers are tough and intelligent; that is the impression we received wherever we met them. Naturally, as we rushed through the country, we were struck most by picturesque details. But even such details can give rise to many conclusions. For example, that the settlers are good horsemen. When we got to Rehovot, a cavalcade of young people came galloping toward us—some twenty men who wanted to escort us to the settlement. On their swift horses they performed a kind of Arabian *fantasia* around our carriages, and we were reminded of the rodeo riders of the Wild West of America when we saw these sturdy, tanned lads turn their horses around, dash away cross-country, and gallop back again amidst shouts of jubilation.

Unfortunately we were able to visit only a small number of settlements, but we did get to know the Jewish farmer. He holds a great deal of promise for the future.

VISIONS FOR PALESTINE

Yes, we continue to believe—and since our visit more firmly than ever—that this country, which is so magnificently endowed by nature, is a land of the future. The enchanting coastline on the blue sea can be turned into a Riviera once the cultural force of a large-scale settlement is brought to bear on it. To be sure, enormous investments will be required to provide the country with all the modern facilities of communications and sanitation. But what elbow-room there is for the active enterprising spirit of a people educated in all the civilized countries and familiar with every modern resource! And what rewards beckon at the end of these simple undertakings! Great investments of labor and capital will be necessary, but in this magnificent region toil will bear golden fruit and capital will reap its profits.

As we hurried past, we saw plains fast becoming fruitful, and beautiful mountain ranges. Everywhere nature and opportunities wait for helping human hands that can and will again create gardens there, places where people can live.

Jerusalem left a powerful impression. Even in its present state of ruin one can see traces of former beauty. And this city of many hills, which in some respect reminds one of Rome, could once again become a magnificent metropolis. Looking down from the Mount of Olives, one can clearly see the future aspect of the city. The entire ancient, holy city should be free of daily traffic. All those unkempt, noisy peddlers should be banned from within these walls that are venerated by all creeds. Workers' dwellings and inexpensive homes should be built in the environs of the city. The markets should be moved from the Old City to suitable spots outside. Thus cleansed, the Old City would be left to the charitable and religious institutions of all creeds which then could amicably divide up this area among themselves. The entire Old City could gradually be reconstructed in its present style, but under salubrious conditions. It would then be a great jewel that could be placed into the rich setting of a modern, elegant city.

Would such a state of affairs not be more worthy of the feelings and better suited to meet the needs of all the people who cherish Jerusalem? Like an open-air field trip, all this becomes crystal-clear when one is on the spot. The nature of our cause is such that we can discuss it frankly with all those interested, one by one. Who would have any serious objections to the progress of civilization on this particular soil? Least of all, we may assume, Turkey, provided that all legitimate concerns are taken into full account—which is our repeatedly stated desire. Without any doubt, the realization of the Zionist plan means an increase in Turkey's power and prosperity. Some aspects of earlier settlements were such as to evoke suspicion and ill will on the part of the Turkish government. But we have always said, and we repeat it now more emphatically than ever, that we would abhor the idea of the infiltration of small groups. No one has the right to abandon these people to an uncertain fate. Only after formal agreements with the Turkish government has settlement a chance to prosper legally. The Jewish people can offer Turkey such benefits that the conclusion of such an agreement would only be a question of time. . . .

JEWS ARE READY TO BUILD PALESTINE

Now we are able to involve an entire people—a people whose existence we are demonstrating through our great Zionist movement, a people that has preserved its age-old affection for this neglected soil, as one continues to have affection for a sick member of one's family. We can proclaim calmly, openly, and without any diplomatic subtleties what we plan to do with this soil, for no one is ready or able to make such sacrifices for the resuscitation of this soil as can the Jewish people. No one will beat us to it, no one will take it away from us, because no one can muster the dedicated human energy, not to mention the money, that the Jews can. In their present situation, the Jews combine the political impotence, which makes them appear as the least dangerous contenders, with the requisite economic power.

We have unfurled our flag: it is already fluttering above the heads of people. We are full of good cheer and firm confidence. And people will understand that we have sufficient reason for this, for we have succeeded in arousing the interest of two rulers in our just cause.

Let no one say or believe that these great men have something unfriendly in mind. In a dreary self-mockery which discredits all of us, some Jews give this interest a malicious interpretation—that the rulers want to be rid of us. But in reality they are motivated by a most magnanimous intention to disseminate culture, provide unfortunate, wandering masses of people with a home, bring prosperity to a neglected region, and through all this effect some increase in mankind's store of happiness and civilization. This is the cause of their interest, and this is how we have most gratefully understood it.

THE UNITED STATES JOINS THE IMPERIALIST POWERS

SCOTT NEARING AND JOSEPH FREEMAN

From 1870 to 1900 European countries seemed to be involved in a race for colonies. Great Britain, France, Germany, Italy, and Belgium all wanted colonies which, they believed, would provide them with raw materials, workers, markets, and important strategic advantages. The race grew so intense that industrialized countries outside of Europe, namely Japan and the United States, also began to build colonial empires.

In the following selection, Scott Nearing and Joseph Freeman argue that the United States became an imperialist power with the Spanish-American War of 1898. Many Americans particularly objected to Spanish control of Cuba, a large and wealthy island that lay only ninety miles off the coast of Florida and which, many argued, lay within the American sphere of interest. As Nearing and Freeman assert, a pretext for war was established when an American naval vessel, the *Maine*, exploded and sank in the harbor at Havana, Cuba. America's rapid victory led not only ultimately to Cuban independence but to direct American control of Spain's other colonial possessions, most importantly the Philippine Islands in Southeast Asia.

Scott Nearing was a prolific author of political and historical works as well as the cofounder of the American Civil Liberties Union. Joseph Freeman was a journalist and political activist.

Excerpted from *Dollar Diplomacy*, by Scott Nearing and Joseph Freeman. Copyright © 1966 by Monthly Review Press. Reprinted by permission of the Monthly Review Foundation.

A merica's emergence as a modern imperialist power became a generally recognized fact with the outbreak of the Spanish-American War, the avowed object of which was the liberation of Cuba from Spanish domination. The interest of the United States in annexing Cuba, it has been pointed out, was as old as the United States. Following the Civil War the chief aim of the State Department in regard to Cuba was the extension of commercial relations with the island and the protection of American interests there. During the Ten Years War from 1868–1878, in which Cuba sought to break away from Spain, the United States threatened to intervene, with the implication of annexing the island. In 1895 Cuba began its final insurrection against Spain, and a bitter struggle followed in which the insurrectionists carried on a guerilla war while the Spaniards herded the population into concentration camps.

In addition to the unbroken interest which the United States had shown toward Cuban annexation for almost a century, American investments in Cuba by 1893 amounted to over $50,000,000; the trade of the United States with the island had reached a value of $100,000,000; while American claims amounted to over $16,000,000. Consequently the McKinley administration, which took office in 1897, began to negotiate with Spain for a cessation of hostilities.

AN AMERICAN SHIP EXPLODES IN CUBA

Spain offered to grant Cuba autonomy, but the insurrectionists insisted on complete independence. On January 13, 1898, a riot took place in Havana as a deliberate demonstration against the plan for autonomy; and the American consul-general advised Washington that a warship might be necessary to protect Americans in Havana. The *Maine* was promptly dispatched and anchored in Havana harbour on January 25. Meantime the Hearst press, which had been carrying on a sensational campaign for war, published a private letter written by the Spanish ambassador at Washington, in which President McKinley was criticised for "keeping on good terms with the jingoes of his party." This letter, according to Secretary of State Day, was "surreptitiously if not criminally obtained." However, it served its purpose; the popular clamour for war increased. On the evening of February 15 the *Maine* blew up in the harbour of Havana, and two officers and 258 men were killed. Although "there was no evidence whatever that any one connected with the exercise of Spanish authority in Cuba had had so much as guilty knowledge of the plans made to destroy the *Maine*" it was assumed that the ship had been blown up by the Spanish, and the demand for war became louder.

Meantime the American Minister at Madrid was discussing the purchase of Cuba by the United States. On March 17, 1898, he wrote to the Secretary of State that "if we have war we must finally occupy and ultimately own the island. If today we could purchase at reasonable price we should avoid the horrors and expense of war." Spain refused to sell; but in response to an offer by President McKinley for an armistice with the Cuban revolutionists and adjustment through the assistance of the United States, the Spanish government offered to submit the question involved in the explosion of the *Maine* to arbitration, and to leave the pacification of the island to a Cuban parliament. Representatives of Germany, Austria-Hungary, France, Great Britain, Italy, and Russia made a formal appeal to President McKinley for peace, and the Pope prevailed upon Spain to suspend hostilities. By this time most of the disputed points between the United States and Spain had been settled; there were no Americans in Cuban prisons; the reconcetrado policy had been stopped; American relief had been admitted on the island; arbitration of the *Maine* incident had been offered; and amnesty had been granted. Nevertheless, President McKinley submitted the question to Congress on April 11 in a message which practically made no mention of Spain's offer of peace.

PRESIDENT MCKINLEY CALLS FOR WAR WITH SPAIN

The president's message and the debates on it in Congress showed that the interest of the United States in the fate of Cuba was not entirely humanitarian. Senators pointed out that "for three-fourths of a century this Government has persistently asserted its right to control the ultimate destiny of Cuba." The message advocated "the forcible intervention of the United States as a neutral to stop the war" on the following grounds:

> First. In the cause of humanity and to put an end to the barbarities, bloodshed, starvation, and horrible miseries now existing there. . . . Second. We owe it to our citizens in Cuba to afford them that protection and indemnity for life and property which no government there can or will afford. . . . Third. The right to intervene may be justified by the very serious injury to the commerce, trade, and business of our people and by the wanton destruction of property, and devastation of the island. Fourth, and which is of the utmost importance. The present condition of affairs in Cuba is a constant menace to our peace, and entails upon this Government an enormous expense.

American "trade has suffered," the message said; "the capital invested by our citizens in Cuba has been largely lost." What McKinley's real intentions toward "Cuba libre [a free Cuba]" were, he indicated in the following words:

> Nor from the standpoint of expediency do I think it would be wise or prudent for this Government to recognize at the present time the independence of the so-called Cuban Republic. Such recognition is not necessary in order to enable the United States to intervene and pacify the island. To commit this country now to the recognition of any particular government in Cuba might subject us to embarrassing conditions of international obligation toward the organization so recognized. In case of intervention our conduct would be subject to the approval or disapproval of such government. We would be required to submit to its direction and to assume to it the mere relation of a friendly ally.

On April 19 Congress passed a joint resolution declaring that "the people of the Island of Cuba are, and of right ought to be, free and independent, and that the Government of the United States hereby recognizes the Republic of Cuba as the true and lawful government of that island," and empowered the President to use the army and navy to carry out the provisions of the resolution. That there were elements in the United States opposed to the annexation of Cuba was indicated by the addition of the Taller amendment which declared that "the United States hereby disclaims any disposition or intention to exercise sovereignty, jurisdiction, or control over said island, except for the pacification thereof, and asserts its determination when that is accomplished to leave the government and control of the island to its people." Two days later President McKinley ordered a blockade of Cuban ports and the war was. on. At the same time Commodore George Dewey, in command of the Asiatic squadron at Hongkong, was ordered to proceed to Manila Bay in the Philippine Islands, which belonged to Spain, and to capture or destroy the Spanish fleet there.

CHINA'S BOXER REBELLION STRIKES AT WESTERN IMPERIALISTS

Diana Preston

At the end of the nineteenth century China, like most of the rest of the world, was dominated by the Western imperial powers. It remained nominally independent under the Ching, or Manchu, emperors, but in reality had been carved into various spheres of interest by European countries as well as Japan and the United States. Foreign businesses took advantage of China's labor and resources, while Christian missionaries aggressively sought converts.

In the following selection, Diana Preston describes how a group of rebels, known as Boxers because of their martial arts practices, tried to rid China of Western imperialists in 1900. The author focuses on the Boxers' siege of the foreign quarter of Peking (Beijing), China's capital, noting that the Ching empress Tzu Hsi hoped to use the Boxer Rebellion to prop up her collapsing authority. Preston also acknowledges that the greatest victims of the rebellion, as well as of the foreign coalition that suppressed it, were the people of China.

Diana Preston's historical works include *The Road to Culloden Moor* and *A First Rate Tragedy: Robert Falcon Scott and the Race to the South Pole*. She is currently working on a book on the sinking of the *Lusitania*.

"**S**tanding together as the sun rose fully, the little remaining band, all Europeans, met death stubbornly. . . . As one man fell others advanced, and finally, overcome by overwhelming odds, every one of the Europeans remaining was put to the sword in a most atrocious manner." So read a dramatic dispatch in the London *Daily Mail* of 16 July 1900 from its special correspondent in Shanghai. Under the headline "The Pekin Massacre," it confirmed in gruesome detail what the world already suspected—that hundreds of foreigners besieged in Peking's diplomatic quarter since 20 June had been murdered.

The news flew around the world, gaining in horrific detail. The *New York Times* dwelt on the fate of the Russian minister and his wife, plunged into boiling oil. It informed its readers that the besieged "went mad and killed all their women and children with revolvers."

In the event, these reports proved false. They might so easily have been true. The summer of 1900 witnessed a pivotal episode in China's fractured relationship with the West—the Boxer rising. It was an event that left tens of thousands dead and touched the lives of millions more. It precipitated the end of the ruling Manchu dynasty. It tainted China's relationship with the wider world, and continues to do so even today.

The Boxer rising prompted an unprecedented international response. It saw the first steps in America's gradual assumption from Britain of the role of an often misunderstood, sometimes misguided, and occasionally hypocritical world policeman. It brought home to Americans the moral compromises—and the cost in human lives—of becoming involved with diversely motivated allies in interventions against hostile populations in distant alien lands. It also revealed Japan's growing confidence and military prowess to a startled world. Soon she would become China's greatest tormentor.

OPPOSITION TO "RICE CHRISTIANS"

The Boxers themselves were an unlikely catalyst for such farreaching effects. An obscure, ill-organized sect that claimed to possess supernatural powers, it drew its members mainly from the poor and dispossessed of northern China. The foreigners called them "Boxers" because of the ritualistic martial arts they practiced. Their lives had long been a losing struggle against cycles of flood, drought, and famine. The arrival in China of increasing numbers of foreigners had only deepened their misery. Some foreigners came in pursuit of commerce, and the new technologies they brought with them—steamboats and locomotives, telegraph systems and mining equipment—not only offended the spirits of earth, water, and air but also robbed many Chinese of their jobs. Christian missionaries—fresh-faced and idealistic men and women from the American Midwest, bearded priests from Germany and France—came in search of souls. Often ignorant, dismissive, or contemptuous of the native culture, they and their aggressive proselytizing threatened the very fabric of Chinese family and village life. The Boxers despised their Chinese converts as traitors, "rice Christians" who had sold themselves for a square meal.

The Boxers' simmering resentment erupted across the northern provinces of Shantung, Shansi, and Chihli in the summer of 1900. Chanting mobs surrounded the mission stations and dragged out their terrorized occupants. Some they killed on the spot; others they took to Boxer temples to be slowly tortured to death. Tens of thousands of Chinese converts, Protestant and Catholic, were murdered—hacked to pieces, skinned alive, set alight, or buried still living.

The Boxers attacked and murdered Western railway engineers and burned down stations. Reinforced by Imperial Chinese troops, they blockaded 600 foreigners and some 4,000 Chinese Christians in the international port of Tientsin. The foreigners in Peking [modern Beijing: China's capital]—nearly 900 men, women, and children from the eighteen most powerful nations in the world—were besieged in the diplomatic quarter. Established in the 1860s following China's defeat in the war with Britain and France, the quarter was by 1900 a commercial as well as a diplomatic district. Banks, shops, and offices prospered alongside the embassies—or "legations," as they were then known—of America, Britain, Russia, Japan, and many of the countries of Western Europe.

The siege forced the quarter's motley population—diplomats and missionaries, academics and adventurers, soldiers and visiting socialites, journalists and engineers—to cooperate despite differences of language and custom and a long history of petty rivalries. The women sewed sandbags of expensive silks, and everyone, from ambassadors' wives to Orthodox priests, filled them. Brave men, both marines and civilian volunteers, fought and died behind them. The cowardly hid in cellars on the flimsiest of excuses. The besieged cooked and ate unappetizing, indigestible meals of rice and horsemeat and were glad of them. Nearly everyone got dysentery. In the heat of the humid Peking summer, thick swarms of black flies and the sickly sweet stench of rotting human flesh were everywhere. The plight of the three thousand or so Chinese converts sheltering in a carefully segregated part of the compound was worst of all. Denied an equal distribution of the food, they were soon reduced to stripping the bark off trees and devouring crows and dogs bloated on human corpses in an effort to survive.

At first everyone listened for the sound of the relief force's guns. When it did not come some men made preparations to shoot their wives and children should the "yellow fiends" overrun the complex. Others smoked cigars and swilled champagne from the well-stocked cellars. A few cracked under the strain and were locked up. The more phlegmatic wondered how they had gotten into a predicament that even the supposed experts had failed to foresee.

In the nearby Peitang Cathedral, a handful of French and Italian guards under the glinting eye of the martial French bishop Favier struggled against frightening odds and in even worse conditions to defend a community of nearly thirty-five hundred souls.

AN AGED EMPRESS LOOKS ON

Watching and waiting on events from within Peking's fabled pink-walled Forbidden City was "the Old Buddha," Tzu Hsi, the sixty-five-year-old Empress Dowager of China. In an otherwise totally male-dominated society, this extraordinary woman had held power, directly or indirectly, for nearly forty years. To many of the foreign community she was an Asiatic Catherine de Medici, a woman of unimaginable sexual appetites and political ambition who murdered anyone, including her closest family, who stood in her way. A reactionary to the core, she had recently incarcerated her nephew the emperor for daring to lead a reform movement. She shared the Boxers' loathing of the foreigners in China and was astute enough to realize two things: First, the Boxers could help her sweep the hated interlopers out of China, and second, their genuine social and economic grievances had to be harnessed or they might be turned against her and the Manchu dynasty. She therefore turned a blind eye to the Boxers' murderous activities, then gave them official support. It proved her greatest mistake.

Foreign troops relieved Tientsin in July while an international relief force eventually raised the sieges of the diplomatic quarter and the Peitang Cathedral in August. By then, however, over 200 foreigners had been killed or wounded in the diplomatic quarter and hundreds of Chinese Christians had perished, most from starvation and disease. In the Peitang over 400 Chinese and foreigners had died, including 166 children. In the Chinese hinterland, some 200 foreign nuns, priests, and missionaries and their families had been murdered while the death toll of Chinese converts ran into tens of thousands. The numbers of Boxers and Imperial troops who perished can only be guessed.

Both Tientsin and Peking were thoroughly and indiscriminately looted by all nationalities and all classes. Many innocent civilians committed suicide rather than face being raped and killed. Moats, rivers, and wells became clogged with bodies. It had been a terrible bloodbath and it had backfired badly on Tzu Hsi. In her final years she was forced to embrace the very reforms she had earlier resisted and indeed to introduce them so quickly that they undermined the dynasty she had fought to preserve. The last emperor, Pu Yi, was deposed in 1911, just three years after her death.

Signs of Uncertainty and Danger as the Century Turns

CHAPTER 4

DREAMS ARE STATEMENTS OF THE SUBCONSCIOUS MIND

SIGMUND FREUD

The age of psychoanalysis began when Sigmund Freud, an Austrian physician, began to concern himself with the forces underlying neurosis and mental illness in the 1890s. He soon developed the idea that many of the problems of the mind derived from childhood and sexual experiences that for whatever reason the conscious mind had repressed. Since the memory of these experiences remained alive in the subconscious mind, Freud sought ways to encourage patients to delve into their subconscious and recover them.

The following selection is from one of Freud's earliest works, *The Interpretation of Dreams*, published in 1905. In it, Freud asserts that dreams can be understood according to the psychoanalytical method he was developing. In it, he encouraged the patient to speak freely, without self-criticism or hindrance, about whatever passed through his or her mind. Freud claimed that since dreams appeared when patients were sleeping and thus incapable of consciously editing or censoring their thoughts, dreams were reflections of an unsuppressed mind.

I must insist that the dream actually does possess a meaning, and that a scientific method of dream-interpretation is possible. I arrived at my knowledge of this method in the following manner:

For years I have been occupied with the resolution of certain

Excerpted from "The Interpretation of Dreams," by Sigmund Freud, in *The Basic Writings of Sigmund Freud*, translated by A.A. Brill. (New York: The Modern Library, 1938).

psycho-pathological structures—hysterical phobias, obsessional ideas, and the like—with therapeutic intentions. I have been so occupied, in fact, ever since I heard the significant statement of Joseph Breuer [a physician and former partner of Freud], to the effect that in these structures, regarded as morbid symptoms, solution and treatment go hand in hand. Where it has been possible to trace a pathological idea back to those elements in the psychic life of the patient to which it owed its origin, this idea has crumbled away, and the patient has been relieved of it. In view of the failure of our other therapeutic efforts, and in the face of the mysterious character of these pathological conditions, it seemed to me tempting, in spite of all the difficulties, to follow the method initiated by Breuer until a complete elucidation of the subject had been achieved. I shall have occasion elsewhere to give a detailed account of the form which the technique of this procedure has finally assumed, and of the results of my efforts. In the course of these psychoan-

Sigmund Freud developed a scientific method of dream interpretation.

alytic studies, I happened upon the question of dream-interpretation. My patients, after I had pledged them to inform me of all the ideas and thoughts which occurred to them in connection with a given theme, related their dreams, and thus taught me that a dream may be interpolated in the psychic concatenation, which may be followed backwards from a pathological idea into the patient's memory. The next step was to treat the dream itself as a symptom, and to apply to it the method of interpretation which had been worked out for such symptoms.

For this a certain psychic preparation on the part of the patient is necessary. A twofold effort is made, to stimulate his attentiveness in respect of his psychic perceptions, and to eliminate the critical spirit in which he is ordinarily in the habit of viewing such thoughts as come to the surface. For the purpose of self-observation with concentrated attention it is advantageous that the patient should take up a restful position and close his eyes; he must be explicitly instructed to renounce all criticism of the thought-formations which he may perceive. He must also be told that the success of the psychoanalysis depends upon his noting and communicating everything that passes through his mind, and that he must not allow himself to suppress one idea because it seems to him unimportant or irrelevant to the subject, or another because it seems nonsensical. He must preserve an absolute impartiality in respect to his ideas; for if he is unsuccessful in finding the desired solution of the dream, the obsessional idea, or the like, it will be because he permits himself to be critical of them.

I have noticed in the course of my psychoanalytical work that the psychological state of a man in an attitude of reflection is entirely different from that of a man who is observing his psychic processes. In reflection there is a greater play of psychic activity than in the most attentive self-observation; this is shown even by the tense attitude and the wrinkled brow of the man in a state of reflection, as opposed to the mimic tranquillity of the man observing himself. In both cases there must be concentrated attention, but the reflective man makes use of his critical faculties, with the result that he rejects some of the thoughts which rise into consciousness after he has become aware of them, and abruptly interrupts others, so that he does not follow the lines of thought which they would otherwise open up for him; while in respect of yet other thoughts he is able to behave in such a manner that they do not become conscious at all—that is to say, they are suppressed before they are perceived. In self-observation, on the other hand, he has but one task—that of suppressing criticism; if he succeeds in doing this, an unlimited number of thoughts enter his consciousness which would otherwise have eluded his grasp. With the aid of the material thus obtained— material which is new to the self-observer—it is possible to achieve the interpretation of pathological ideas, and also that of dream-formations. As will be seen, the point is to induce a psychic state which is in some degree analogous, as regards the distribution of psychic energy (mobile attention), to the state of the mind before falling asleep—and also, of course, to the hypnotic state. On falling asleep the "undesired ideas" emerge, owing to the slackening of a certain arbitrary (and, of course, also critical) action, which is allowed to influence the trend of our ideas; we are accustomed to speak of fatigue as the reason of this slackening; the emerging undesired ideas are changed into visual and auditory images. In the condition which it utilized for the analysis of dreams and pathological ideas, this activity is purposely and deliberately renounced, and the psychic energy thus saved (or some part of it) is employed in attentively tracking the undesired thoughts which now come to the surface—thoughts which retain their identity as ideas (in which the condition differs from the state of falling asleep). "Undesired ideas" are thus changed into "desired" ones.

ALBERT EINSTEIN BECOMES A SCIENTIFIC CELEBRITY

BANESH HOFFMANN AND HELEN DUKAS

In the following selection Banesh Hoffmann and Helen Dukas argue that physicist Albert Einstein, whose theory of relativity was first published in 1905, possessed a special kind of genius. While he was a creative and talented scientist, he possessed in addition a "magic touch" that not only altered scientific thought but also made him famous. Such renown was bewildering to Einstein, who was born humbly in Ulm, Germany, and developed his ideas while an employee in a patent office in Bern, Switzerland.

The authors also point out that Einstein's theory of relativity, which demonstrated that the understanding of time and space, as well as the various characteristics of whatever was being measured, was relative to the observer, was part of a larger revolution in physics. This scientific revolution was to lead, ultimately, to such twentieth-century phenomena as the atomic bomb.

Banesh Hoffmann was historian of science at Queen's College, Oxford. Helen Dukas worked as Einstein's private archivist after 1928.

He is, of course, best known for his theory of relativity, which brought him world fame. But with fame came a form of near-idolatry that Albert Einstein found incomprehensible. To his amazement, he became a living legend, a veritable folk hero, looked upon as an oracle, entertained by royalty, statesmen, and other celebrities, and treated by public and press

Excerpted from "The Man and the Child," by Banesh Hoffmann and Helen Dukas, in *Albert Einstein: Creator and Rebel*. Copyright © 1972 by Helen Dukas and Banesh Hoffmann. Reprinted with permission from Dutton, a division of Penguin Putnam, Inc.

as if he were a movie star rather than a scientist. When, in Hollywood's glittering heyday, Chaplin took Einstein to the gala opening of his film *City Lights,* the crowds surged around the limousine as much to gape at Einstein as at Chaplin. Turning in bewilderment to his host, Einstein asked, "What does it mean?" to which the worldly-wise Chaplin bitterly replied, "Nothing."

Though fame brought its inevitable problems, it had no power to spoil Einstein; vanity was no part of him. He showed no trace of pomposity or exaggerated self-importance. Journalists pestered him with irrelevancies and inanities. Painters, sculptors, and photographers, famous and obscure, came in a steady stream to make his portrait. Yet through it all he retained his simplicity and his sense of humor. When a passenger on a train, not recognizing him, asked him his occupation, he ruefully replied, "I am an artists' model." Harassed by requests for his autograph, he remarked to friends that autograph hunting was the last vestige of cannibalism: people used to eat people, but now they sought symbolic pieces of them instead. After being lionized at a social affair, he confided dolefully, "When I was young, all I wanted and expected from life was to sit quietly in some corner doing my work without the public paying attention to me. And now see what has become of me."

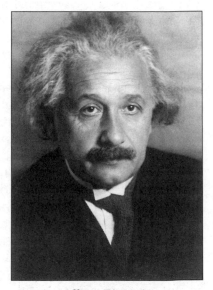

Albert Einstein

Long before the public heard of him, Einstein's importance had been recognized by physicists. His theory of relativity has two main parts, the special theory and the general. Not till just after World War I, when eclipse observations lent confirmation to a prediction of the general theory of relativity, did word leak out to the public that something momentous had happened in the world of science.

EINSTEIN WAS PART OF A REVOLUTION IN SCIENCE

Einstein came at a time of unprecedented crisis in physics. Relativity was not the only revolutionary scientific development of the early twentieth century. The quantum revolution, which is also part of our story, developed more or less simultaneously and was even more radical than relativity. Yet it made no such public splash and produced no such popular hero as did the latter.

The myth arose that in the whole world only a half-dozen scientists were capable of understanding the general theory of relativity. When Einstein first propounded the theory this may well have been no great exaggeration. But even after dozens of authors had written articles and books explaining the theory, the myth did not die. It has had a long life and traces of it survive even now, when according to a recent estimate the year's output of significant published articles involving the general theory of relativity is somewhere in the neighborhood of seven hundred to a thousand.

The myth and the eclipse observations gave the theory an aura of mystery and cosmic serenity that must have caught the fancy of a war-weary public eager to forget the guilt and horror of World War I. Yet, even when looked at plain, the theory of relativity remains a towering achievement. In a letter written when he had just turned fifty-one, Einstein indicated that he regarded this theory as his true lifework and said of his other concepts that he looked on them more as *Gelegenheitsarbeit*—work performed as the occasion arose. . . .

Carl Seelig, one of Einstein's chief biographers, once wrote to him asking whether he inherited his scientific gift from his father's side and his musical from his mother's. Einstein replied in all sincerity, I have no special gift—I am only passionately curious. Thus it is not a question of heredity." In saying this, Einstein was not being coy. Rather, he was being careful. He was responding as best he could to an ill-conceived question. If we imagine that it referred to Einstein's scientific artistry, we read into it something that Seelig surely did not have in mind. Implicitly the question put Einstein's music on a par with his science. True, Einstein loved music and played the violin better than many an amateur. But was he, in music, comparable to his favorite composer, Mozart, as in science he was comparable to Newton, whom he revered?

In science Einstein was certainly no amateur. His talents were of thoroughly professional caliber. To the layman the talents of an outstanding professional in any field, whether theology or forgery, can well seem awe-inspiring, But talent is no great rarity, and by professional standards Einstein's scientific talent and technical skill were not spectacular. They were surpassed by those of many a competent practitioner. In this strict sense, then, Einstein indeed had no special scientific gift. What he did have that was special was the magic touch without which even the most passionate curiosity would be ineffectual: he had the authentic magic that transcends logic and distinguishes the genius from the mass of lesser men with greater talent.

EUROPEAN CIVILIZATION IS A SHAM

GEORGE BERNARD SHAW

At the turn of the twentieth century most Europeans were convinced that their civilization represented unquestioned human progress. English playwright George Bernard Shaw, on the other hand, asserted that European civilization was violent, barbaric, and hypocritical. The following passage, in which he makes these claims, is taken from "The Revolutionist's Handbook," a pamphlet included in published versions of Shaw's play *Man and Superman*.

Shaw makes numerous historical comparisons with the world of his own day to support his claim that European progress was a myth. Despite the pageantry of imperialism, Shaw argues that imperialists often use arbitrary violence and even torture to achieve their ends. And despite the material wealth created by industrialism, Shaw notes that industrial cities are filthy and workers exploited and humiliated. Even medicine, religion, and education, Shaw complains, reflect the hypocrisy of those who preach progress.

George Bernard Shaw's most famous plays include *Pygmalion*, *Caesar and Cleopatra*, and *Saint Joan*.

A fter all, the progress illusion is not so very subtle. We begin by reading the satires of our fathers' contemporaries; and we conclude (usually quite ignorantly) that the abuses exposed by them are things of the past. We see also that reforms of crying evils are frequently produced by the sectional

Excerpted from "The Revolutionist's Handbook," in *Man and Superman,* by George Bernard Shaw (Cambridge, MA: Harvard University Press, 1903).

shifting of political power from oppressors to oppressed. The poor man is given a vote by the Liberals in the hope that he will cast it for his emancipators. The hope is not fulfilled; but the life-long imprisonment of penniless men for debt ceases; Factory Acts are passed to mitigate sweating [hard labor]; schooling is made free and compulsory; sanitary by-laws are multiplied; public steps are taken to house the masses decently; the bare-footed get boots; rags become rare; and bathrooms and pianos, smart tweeds and starched collars, reach numbers of people who once, as "the unsoaped," played the Jew's harp or the accordion in moleskins and belchers. Some of these changes are gains: some of them are losses. Some of them are not changes at all: all of them are merely the changes that money makes. Still, they produce an illusion of bustling progress; and the reading class infers from them that the abuses of the early Victorian period no longer exist except as amusing pages in the novels of Dickens.

THE INCOMPETENCE OF MODERN GOVERNMENT

But the moment we look for a reform due to character and not to money, to statesmanship and not to interest or mutiny, we are disillusioned. For example, we remembered the maladministration and incompetence revealed by the Crimean War as part of a bygone state of things until the South African war showed that the nation and the War Office, like those poor Bourbons who have been so impudently blamed for a universal characteristic, had learnt nothing and forgotten nothing. We had hardly recovered from the fruitless irritation of this discovery when it transpired that the officers' mess of our most select regiment included a flogging club presided over by the senior subaltern. The disclosure provoked some disgust at the details of this schoolboyish debauchery, but no surprise at the apparent absence of any conception of manly honor and virtue, of personal courage and self-respect, in the front rank of our chivalry. In civil affairs we had assumed that the sycophancy and idolatry which encouraged Charles I to undervalue the Puritan revolt of the seventeenth century had been long outgrown; but it has needed nothing but favorable circumstances to revive, with added abjectness to compensate for its lost piety. We have relapsed into disputes about transubstantiation at the very moment when the discovery of the wide prevalence of theophagy [sightings of God] as a tribal custom has deprived us of the last excuse for believing that our official religious rites differ in essentials from those of barbarians. The Christian doctrine of the uselessness of punishment and the wickedness of revenge has not, in spite of its simple common sense, found a single convert among the nations:

Christianity means nothing to the masses but a sensational public execution which is made an excuse for other executions. In its
name we take ten years of a thief's life minute by minute in the
slow misery and degradation of modern reformed imprisonment
with as little remorse as Laud and his Star Chamber clipped the
ears of Bastwick and Burton.

THE CRUELTY OF EMPIRE

We dug up and mutilated the remains of the Mahdi [the king of
the Sudan] the other day exactly as we dug up and mutilated the
remains of Cromwell two centuries ago. We have demanded the
decapitation of the Chinese Boxer princes as any Tartar would
have done; and our military and naval expeditions to kill, burn,
and destroy tribes and villages for knocking an Englishman on
the head are so common a part of our Imperial routine that the
last dozen of them has not elicited as much sympathy as can be
counted on by any lady criminal. The judicial use of torture to ex-
tort confession is supposed to be a relic of darker ages; but whilst
these pages are being written an English judge has sentenced a
forger to twenty years' penal servitude with an open declaration
that the sentence will be carried out in full unless he confesses
where he has hidden the notes he forged. And no comment
whatever is made either on this or on a telegram from the seat of
war in Somaliland mentioning that certain information has been
given by a prisoner of war "under punishment." Even if these reports were false, the fact that they are accepted without protest
as indicating a natural and proper course of public conduct
shows that we are still as ready to resort to torture as Bacon was.
As to vindictive cruelty, an incident in the South African war,
when the relatives and friends of a prisoner were forced to wit-
ness his execution, betrayed a baseness of temper and character
which hardly leaves us the right to plume ourselves on our superiority to Edward III at the surrender of Calais. And the democratic American officer indulges in torture in the Philippines just
as the aristocratic English officer did in South Africa. The incidents of the white invasion of Africa in search of ivory, gold, di-
amonds and sport, have proved that the modern European is the
same beast of prey that formerly marched to the conquest of new
worlds under Alexander, Antony, and Pizarro. Parliaments and
vestries are just what they were when Cromwell suppressed
them and Dickens ridiculed them. The democratic politician remains exactly as Plato described him; the physician is still the
credulous impostor and petulant scientific coxcomb whom
Molière ridiculed; the schoolmaster remains at best a pedantic
child farmer and at worst a flagellomaniac; arbitrations are more

dreaded by honest men than lawsuits; the philanthropist is still a parasite on misery as the doctor is on disease; the miracles of priestcraft are none the less fraudulent and mischievous because they are now called scientific experiments and conducted by professors; witchcraft, in the modern form of patent medicines and prophylactic inoculations, is rampant; the landowner who is no longer powerful enough to set the mantrap of Rhampsinitis [a poison] improves on it by barbed wire; the modern gentleman who is too lazy to daub his face with vermilion as a symbol of bravery employs a laundress to daub his shirt with starch as a symbol of cleanliness; we shake our heads at the dirt of the Middle Ages in cities made grimy with soot and foul and disgusting with shameless tobacco smoking; holy water, in its latest form of disinfectant fluid, is more widely used and believed in than ever; public health authorities deliberately go through incantations with burning sulphur (which they know to be useless) because the people believe in it as devoutly as the Italian peasant believes in the liquefaction of the blood of St. Januarius; and straightforward public lying has reached gigantic developments, there being nothing to choose in this respect between the pickpocket at the police station and the minister on the treasury bench, the editor in the newspaper office, the city magnate advertising bicycle tires that do not side-slip, the clergyman subscribing the thirty-nine articles, and the vivisector who pledges his knightly honor that no animal operated on in the physiological laboratory suffers the slightest pain.

AN AGE OF HYPOCRITES

Hypocrisy is at its worst; for we not only persecute bigotedly but sincerely in the name of the cure-mongering witchcraft we do believe in, but callously and hypocritically in the name of the Evangelical creed that our rulers privately smile at as the Italian patricians of the fifth century smiled at Jupiter and Venus. Sport is, as it has always been, murderous excitement: the impulse to slaughter is universal; and museums are set up throughout the country to encourage little children and elderly gentlemen to make collections of corpses preserved in alcohol, and to steal birds' eggs and keep them as the red Indian used to keep scalps. Coercion with the lash is as natural to an Englishman as it was to Solomon spoiling Rehoboam: indeed, the comparison is unfair to the Jews in view of the facts that the Mosaic law forbade more than forty lashes in the name of humanity, and that floggings of a thousand lashes were inflicted on English soldiers in the eighteenth and nineteenth centuries, and would be inflicted still but for the change in the balance of political power between the military caste and the commercial classes and the proletariat. In spite of that change, flogging is still an institution in the public school, in the military prison, on the training ship, and in that school of littleness called the home. The lascivious clamor of the flagellomaniac for more of it, constant as the clamor for more insolence, more war, and lower rates, is tolerated and even gratified because, having no moral ends in view, we have sense enough to see that nothing but brute coercion can impose our selfish will on others. Cowardice is universal: patriotism, public opinion, parental duty, discipline, religion, morality, are only fine names for intimidation; and cruelty, gluttony, and credulity keep cowardice in countenance. We cut the throat of a calf and hang it up by the heels to bleed to death so that our veal cutlet may be white; we nail geese to a board and cram them with food because we like the taste of liver disease; we tear birds to pieces to decorate our women's hats; we mutilate domestic animals for no reason at all except to follow an instinctively cruel fashion; and we connive at the most abominable tortures in the hope of discovering some magical cure for our own diseases by them.

All that can be said for us is that people must and do live and let live up to a certain point. Even the horse, with his docked tail and bitted jaw, finds his slavery mitigated by the fact that a total disregard of his need for food and rest would put his master to the expense of buying a new horse every second day; for you cannot work a horse to death and then pick up another one for nothing, as you can a laborer. But this natural check on inconsiderate selfishness is itself checked, partly by our shortsightedness, and partly by deliberate calculation; so that beside the man who, to his own loss, will shorten his horse's life in mere stinginess, we have the tramway company which discovers actuarially that though a horse may live from 24 to 40 years, yet it pays better to work him to death in 4 and then replace him by a fresh victim. And human slavery, which has reached its worst recorded point within our own time in the form of free wage labor, has encountered the same personal and commercial limits to both its aggravation and its mitigation. Now that the freedom of wage labor has produced a scarcity of it, as in South Africa, the leading English newspaper and the leading English weekly review have openly and without apology demanded a return to compulsory labor: that is, to the methods by which, as we believe, the Egyptians built the pyramids. We know now that the crusade against chattel slavery in the nineteenth century succeeded solely because chattel slavery was neither the most effective nor the least humane method of labor exploitation; and the world is now feeling its way towards a still more effective system which shall abolish the freedom of the worker without again making his exploiter responsible for him as a chattel.

THE WORLD'S FEW "SUPERMEN"

Still, there is always some mitigation: there is the fear of revolt; and there are the effects of kindliness and affection. Let it be repeated therefore that no indictment is here laid against the world on the score of what its criminals and monsters do. The fires of Smithfield and of the Inquisition were lighted by earnestly pious people, who were kind and good as kindness and goodness go. And when a Negro is dipped in kerosene and set on fire in America at the present time, he is not a good man lynched by ruffians: he is a criminal lynched by crowds of respectable, charitable, virtuously indignant, high-minded citizens, who, though they act outside the law, are at least more merciful than the American legislators and judges who not so long ago condemned men to solitary confinement for periods, not of five months, as our own practice is, but of five years and more. The things that our moral monsters do may be left out of account with St. Bartholomew massacres [in sixteenth-century France] and other momentary outbursts of social disorder. Judge us by the admitted and respected practice of our most reputable circles; and, if you know the facts and are strong enough to look them in the face, you must admit that unless we are replaced by a more highly evolved animal—in short, by the Superman—the world must remain a den of dangerous animals among whom our few accidental supermen, our Shakespeares, Goethes, Shelleys and their like, must live as precariously as lion tamers do, taking the humor of their situation, and the dignity of their superiority, as a set-off to the horror of the one and the loneliness of the other.

THE WRIGHT BROTHERS INAUGURATE THE AGE OF FLIGHT

MARVIN W. MCFARLAND

Nineteenth-century innovations in transportation rapidly followed one upon another, especially toward the end of the century. Railroads and steamships provided large-scale transport and acted as engines for both economic growth and technical change. The "safety" bicycle, equipped with pneumatic tires and brakes, swept much of the developed world in the 1880s and 1890s thanks to its affordability and obvious advantages over horses. And by the late 1880s automobiles had appeared, although their role as the dominant mode of transport remained decades in the future.

In the following selection Marvin W. McFarland asserts that the final stage of this era of transportation innovations, the invention of flight, should be credited to two American brothers, Wilbur and Orville Wright. The Wright brothers successfully flew their machine in 1903, and demonstrated, according to McFarland, an energy and intelligence that made them more than mere bicycle mechanics, as some have claimed.

As a captain in the U.S. Air Force, Marvin W. McFarland served as chief archivist to the U.S. Strategic Air Forces in Europe. He is the editor of two volumes of Wright Brothers papers and letters.

Excerpted from "Wilbur and Orville Wright: Seventy-Five Years Later," by Marvin W. Mc-Farland, in *The Wright Bothers: Heirs of Prometheus,* edited by Richard P. Hallion. Copyright © 1978 by the Smithsonian Institution. Reprinted with permission from the Smithsonian National Air and Space Museum.

On December 14, 1903, the Wrights made the first trial of their power machine at Kill Devil Hills, North Carolina. Wilbur won the toss of the coin and got the first turn. It was an abortive flight, the track being laid down the hill, and the pilot made an error of judgment at the start. Nevertheless, the airplane traveled one hundred twelve feet and the power and control were proved ample. The telegram the boys sent their father, Bishop Milton Wright, the next day ended with the words: "Success assured, Keep quiet.". . .

The Wrights began to study the problem of flight deliberately. That is not to say that they were not fascinated by other matters; they were. But they looked around rather cold-bloodedly for something they could sink their teeth into and bring to completion or near-completion. The steamship and the use of metal in constructing ships were accomplished facts. The submarine had been invented. Trains of cars were drawn at speed by steam locomotives on steel rails. The electric light and the telephone were realities. Talking machines with megaphone speakers graced many homes. Wireless telegraphy was in being. The automobile was an increasingly popular and efficient means of transportation, and the improved bicycle produced a craze to which they themselves had succumbed. New rifled guns, cannon, and trinitrotoluene—TNT—were making big war thinkable if not inevitable. The balloon, though not yet the dirigible, had proven its use for conveying messages, some in microform. The modern world was essentially in place. Virtually only the heavier-than-air flying machine remained an unsolved—and some said an insoluble—problem. To unravel this enigma was grist for the Wrights' mill.

The Wrights never claimed to be going at the thing *ab initio* [without initiation]. They made no such pretension. Many aspects of the problem were solved; many others were believed solved. Wilbur, the natural but self-appointed spokesman of the duo, wrote on May 30, 1899, to the Smithsonian Institution:

> I am an enthusiast, but not a crank in the sense that I have some pet theories as to the proper construction of a flying machine. I wish to avail myself of all that is already known and then if possible add my mite to help on the future worker who will attain final success.

With less naiveté Wilbur wrote his father on September 3, 1900, on the eve of departing for Kitty Hawk for the first time:

> It is my belief that flight is possible and while I am taking up the investigation for pleasure rather than profit, I think there is a slight chance of achieving fame and

During the final stage of significant innovations in transportation, the Wright brothers successfully flew their power machine in 1903, sparking the age of flight.

> fortune from it. It is almost the only great problem which has not been pursued by a multitude of investigators, and therefore carried to a point where further progress is very difficult. I am certain I can reach a point much in advance of any previous workers in this field even if complete success is not attained at present.

That the Wrights were tinkerers, bicycle mechanics who struck it lucky and built an airplane that flew, are charges it is painful to have brought against them. . . . It is little short of disgraceful that anyone anywhere in the world can entertain such nonsensical thoughts today.

Atop the Big Kill Devil Hill stands the Wright Memorial monument, erected by the American people during the lifetime of Orville Wright, the only instance of a national monument being put up while one of the persons to whom it is dedicated was still alive. National monuments do not memorialize tinkerers, however clever. Around the pylon are inscribed the words:

> In commemoration of the conquest of the air by the brothers Wilbur and Orville Wright. Conceived by genius. Achieved by dauntless resolution and unconquerable faith.

FROM PEEP-SHOWS TO ONSCREEN THEATRE: THE MOTION PICTURE

ARTHUR KNIGHT

In the following article, film historian Arthur Knight traces the early development of perhaps the most popular form of mass entertainment of the twentieth century: the motion picture. Various persons understood that viewing pictures in rapid succession would give the illusion of motion by the early 1800s, but a number of technological innovations were necessary to produce "movies." Among them was photography itself, developed in the 1830s and 1840s, and, thanks to George Eastman's Kodak camera of 1888, a common facet of life. Another was celluloid film, a problem also solved by the 1880s. Finally, although many others were at work on similar projects, Thomas Edison and his assistant William Dickson invented a machine, the Kinetoscope, which could transmit motion pictures. Edison built his first film studio in 1893.

Knight notes, however, that movies remained a novelty item confined to peep-show parlors and stage-show warmups until filmmakers learned how to tell stories. This involved the use of such techniques as film editing and varied camera angles, and it resulted in *The Great Train Robbery* in 1903, which many consider the first true motion picture.

Arthur Knight taught film studies at the City University of New York.

C ertainly, it was the enthusiasm of the audiences back in 1895, when Edison in America, Lumière in France and Paul in England first threw a moving picture onto a white sheet, that made their novelty something more than an eight-day wonder. To the inventors, the movies were a scientific toy, just one in a long series of devices exploiting the scientific discoveries of the 19th century. To the public, they were a revelation. It was not merely the fact that movement and the shadow of the real world were captured by these machines—that had been done before—but now everything could be seen as large as life and, curiously, even more real. The first audiences sat entranced by such commonplace views as waves dashing to the shore, fire engines racing through the streets, trains drawing into a station, military parades or even people out walking in the sun. But they moved! And they were real! As far as the inventors were concerned, the movies might have remained at that stage—brief one-minute views of the world around us that exploited the novelty of movement. It was the showmen who transformed the novelty into a form of entertainment; and the directors, cameramen and actors, drawn to the medium from all walks of life and all over the world, who transformed it even further from a simple entertainment into an art. . . .

THOMAS EDISON'S KINETOSCOPE

But the most telling contributions to the development of a motion-picture camera unquestionably came from Thomas Edison and his talented assistant, William Kennedy Laurie Dickson. In 1888, after more than a decade of experiment, Edison produced the phonograph, an instrument for recording and playing back sound on wax cylinders. He had already seen the motion photographs of Muybridge, and the idea of combining moving pictures with sound seems to have been in his mind even before the perfected phonograph was offered to the public. In fact, his first efforts in this direction consisted of a strip of small photographs wrapped spirally about just such a cylinder. "Everything should come out of one hole," Edison maintained. When this failed, Edison turned the project over to Dickson—and with it a new film base developed by George Eastman, thin strips of clear, supple, strong celluloid coated with a photographic emulsion. The film began arriving in August of 1889. It was Dickson who solved the mechanical problem of moving it through the camera, devising the sprocket system that is still standard on 35mm film today. Indeed, this ingenious man even managed to link up the pictures with the phonograph, demonstrating the Kinetoscope to his employer on October 6, 1889, with a brief film in which Dickson both appeared and spoke. What was in all probability the first actual presentation of a motion-picture film also marked the debut of the talkies!

Edison's earliest efforts, however, were not directed toward movie projection. He had had considerable success with his penny-in-the-slot phonographs, and it was his opinion that a similar device, offering a brief picture at a penny a look, would ensure a steady profit for his invention. The Kinetoscope was a peep show in which ran a continuous loop of film about 50 feet long. For the moment the sound aspects were ignored as Edison and his crew concentrated on supplying little one-minute subjects for these machines—photographed in the "Black Maria," the world's first film studio, which he built near his West Orange laboratories in 1893. By the fall of 1894, peep-show parlors had sprouted all over the United States and soon appeared in Europe as well. Curiously enough, the inventor seems to have had little confidence in the long-range possibilities of his machine. When in 1891 he took out patents on his battery-driven camera and Kinetoscope, he neglected to pay the additional $150 that would have secured him an international copyright. Within the next few years he was to regret this oversight. In England, Robert W. Paul copied the Edison Kinetoscope and also produced a hand-cranked portable camera. (Edison's first camera had the general shape and weight of a small upright piano.) In France the Lumière brothers, Louis and Auguste, saw the Kinetoscope and promptly invented their own Cinématographe, a machine that not only took pictures but could also print and project them as well. In Berlin, Max and Emil Skladanowski, also inspired by the Edison novelty, produced their Bioskop. These machines were soon to become a serious threat to Edison's market within the United States.

Thus, within fifty years of Roget's presentation of his theory ["The Persistence of Vision with Regard to Moving Objects"], the theory had not only been recognized but its principle had been incorporated into various forms of entertainment. Animation, photography, projection—each was an indispensable step toward the final emergence of the movies. Significantly, none of these steps was taken in any single country. Roget read his paper before the Royal Society in London. Faraday in England, von Stampfer in Austria, Plateau in Belgium all experimented with the idea, producing the various toys and devices that incorporated its principle. Uchatius, who first projected painted pictures, was a Viennese; Désvignes, inventor of the popular toy Zoëtrope, lived in Paris. Both Sellers and Heyl were Americans. Photography, developed in France, was carried forward by Talbot in England and, immeasurably, by George Eastman in this country. There were no secrets, and everything was pointing in one direction—the projection of moving pictures upon a large screen. It should come as no surprise, then, to discover that the movies were actually invented almost simultaneously in France, England, Germany and the United States. The only wonder is that film historians so often seek to establish priority for the inventors of their own countries, resorting to such dubious phrases as "first accredited showing," "first scientific demonstration" or "first public presentation" to bolster their claims. How much better to recognize the indisputable fact that from the very outset the movies were international, that within a single year films were being projected in New York, London, Berlin, Brussels and Paris.

THE FIRST SHOWINGS

Once the Europeans had grasped the principles behind Edison's Kinetoscope, they moved directly toward projecting their pictures on a large screen. In the United States too, other inventors— Eugene Lauste, the Lathams, Jean Le Roy, Thomas Armat and F. Charles Jenkins—were also building machines that would project the Edison Kinetoscope reels. Throughout 1895 there were demonstrations of their equipment in New York, Boston, Chicago, Norfolk and Atlanta. Only Edison held back. When, somewhat belatedly, he finally turned to the problems of projection, he borrowed freely (as bitter law suits subsequently revealed) from the discoveries of Le Roy and Latham, and joined forces with Armat whose Vitascope incorporated the essential Maltese Cross movement to hold the film strip momentarily at rest in the aperture of the projector. Even so, not until April 23, 1896, was Edison prepared to present his projecting Kinetoscope to the public. The presentation took place during the vaudeville program at Koster & Bial's Music Hall, 34th Street and Broadway, the present site of the Macy store. A few months later the American Biograph, Edison's keenest rival, made its debut at Hammerstein's Olympia Music Hall. Within the year, movies were being seen in virtually every large city throughout the United States and Europe.

There is an odd and at the same time important observation to be made about the first films from the two continents. In Europe, Lumière, Pathé, Gaumont and the others delighted primarily in movement for its own sake. Anything that moved was grist for their photographic mills—a laborer felling a wall, workers leaving a factory, a baby eating breakfast in the garden. As their cameramen wandered even farther afield, they took views of ordinary street scenes, of native dances and military parades

wherever they happened to be. The early European film cata-
logues are crowded with *actualités* [scenes of daily life] and brief
documentaires [documentaries], none of them running over a
minute in length, which reflected this intense interest in the world
around them. In America, on the other hand, the actualities were
apt to be of a more sensational sort—the Empire or Black Diamond Express rounding a bend and pounding down the track toward the camera, prize fights, cockfights, Professor Sandow flex-
ing his muscles or Annie Oakley shooting clay pigeons. Even
greater emphasis was placed on bits of staged business—
vaudeville and circus turns, glimpses from plays, novelty acts by
dancers, jugglers and acrobats. Much of the shooting was actually done in studios such as the "Black Maria," or on the impro-
vised stages that had begun to sprout on rooftops all over New
York. In America, at least, the film was firmly linked to a theatrical tradition from the very outset. . . .

MOVING FROM THE STAGE TO THE SCREEN

At this point the movies made their bow, achieving so readily, so
naturally the kind of effects that theater managers could only
dream of. Obviously, this did not mean the end of the theater. Indeed, we find in the early years of the 20th century that the producers in the big cities began to outdo themselves, trying to cram
even more spectacle and greater realism onto the stage than ever
before. Such plays as *Ben Hur, The Light That Failed, Ramona* and
Judith of Bethulia were all huge, heavily mounted, prodigally populated pageants, filled with theatrical devices intended to thrill
their audiences. Appearing only a few years after the introduction of the film, however, the very illusion of reality that they
sought most ingeniously to create on the stage was what the critics attacked most vehemently. Singling out the chariot race from
Ben Hur as an example, one critic wrote in 1899, "The only way
to secure the exact sense of action for this incident in a theater is
to represent it by Mr. Edison's invention."

Gradually, the producers began to forsake spectacular specta-
cles for a somewhat less vast and more detailed realism in their
dramas, melodramas and comedies. Belasco reproduced a section of a Childs Restaurant for a scene in his production of *The
Governor's Lady*. For the second act of *Brewster's Millions* the entire midships of a yacht was created on the stage, complete with
mast, flapping sails and steam whistle; or, for another production, a butcher shop right down to fresh, bleeding carcasses of
beef. Even so, audiences that patronized the theater primarily for
its visual effects continued to desert to the new medium—and
especially in the smaller cities. By the twenties the theater had

bowed to the inevitable, turning to expressionism or impressionism to reinforce the mood of the play. In the field of realism, the upstart movies had won hands down.

Even the crudest, most rudimentary early pictures reflect this superiority. *Mary Stuart,* a popular stage drama of the 1880's, reached its climax, naturally enough, as the headsman lowered his ax on Mary's neck. Out of consideration for the actress playing Mary, the curtain was customarily lowered somewhat faster. One of Edison's first Kinetoscope subjects was *The Execution of Mary, Queen of Scots* (1893). This little film, running just under a minute, begins as Mary approaches the chopping block. She kneels, the headsman swings his ax—and the audience is rewarded with the edifying spectacle of Mary's head rolling in the dust! At the crucial moment, of course, the film was stopped in the camera and a dummy substituted for Mary; but the gruesome bit of action continues on the screen without interruption. When the great Joseph Jefferson consented to do scenes from his stage success *Rip Van Winkle* for the Biograph camera in 1896, his theater performance was photographed in a real forest. This difference between stage and screen is perhaps best pointed up in the popular *May Irwin–John C. Rice Kiss* (1896), a scene from the play *The Widow Jones.* Its few moments of magnified osculation resulted in the first scandalized attempt at film censorship. The "kiss" may have been harmless enough in the theater, but seen in full close-up it suddenly became so much more "real."

It was this element of reality that captured for film its first audiences, the novelty of seeing real things in motion. And there is no doubting that they accepted the flat, flickering images as reality. When locomotives thundered down the track, when waves rolled toward the camera, people in the front rows ran screaming for the exits. Soon, however—all too soon—the novelty began to wear thin. The incessant parades, the street scenes, the acrobats, the butterfly dancers and the onrushing trains lost their appeal. The film could make things move, but then what? By the turn of the century, Mr. Edison's invention—along with the Bioscope, the Cinématographe and the Vitascope—had been relegated to the position of "chaser" on the vaudeville bills, the act that would clear out the theater for the next show. They became the last stop in the tour of the wax museums and the penny-arcades. Other means had to be found to interest audiences. One showman thought he could solve the problem in a purely mechanical way, installing his projector at the far end of a rocking railway coach and presenting scenic views taken from a moving train. These *Hale's Tours* became a craze, somewhat like miniature golf, and made a fortune for their entrepreneur—

but they lasted only a few years. Other movie makers, like J. Stuart Blackton and Albert Smith of the enterprising Vitagraph Corporation, suspected that headline news might bolster interest in the movies. The Boer and the Spanish-American wars afforded Smith a splendid opportunity to test this theory; and an event that he couldn't cover as an eyewitness reporter, like the sinking of the *Maine,* he staged in a bathtub! Still the public's enthusiasm for pictures continued to wane.

Dawn of the Narrative Film: Méliès and Porter

What finally saved the movies was the introduction of narrative. In France, Georges Méliès, a professional magician who early became intrigued with the movie camera, was soon combining his magic tricks with pantomimed stories. His *Cinderella* (1900), *Red Riding Hood* (1901) and *Bluebeard* (1901), and above all his celebrated *A Trip to the Moon* (1902), antedated our own *The Great Train Robbery* (1903) in demonstrating the narrative powers of the new medium. In September of 1899 he filmed an extended account of *L'Affaire Dreyfus,* following it with such serious works as *Jeanne d'Arc* (1900), *The Eruption of Mont-Pelé* (1902) and *The Coronation of Edward VII* (1902), all of them created in his fabulous glass-enclosed little studio on the outskirts of Paris. In these and hundreds of others Méliès, always the magician at heart, exploited not only the narrative but also the trick possibilities of the motion-picture camera. He quickly learned how to stop it in the middle of a scene and create miraculous appearances, disappearances and transformations. He mastered the techniques of double exposure and superimposition, producing truly extraordinary effects. A painter as well, he often designed settings that were triumphs of ingenuity, suggesting through forced perspective, great vistas despite his tiny stage. He was without question the movies' first creative artist.

But Méliès, like so many of his contemporaries, remained chained to the traditions of the theater. In his hands the camera was made to perform wonderful tricks, but they were tricks ingeniously prepared for it on his specially equipped stage. In *A Trip to the Moon,* for example, to create the effect of the rocket ship en route, Méliès hauled a papier-mâché model of the moon up an elaborately constructed ramp toward the camera. It was as if the camera were the sole spectator at an elaborate pageant or play, occupying the choicest seat in the house but never budging from that seat. Everything happens in his films just about as it would on the stage. The actors come on the scene either from the rear or from the wings. Action is arranged horizontally across the stage. Even his trick of merging one scene into the next Méliès adapted from existing stage techniques, making each scene appear to grow out of the last by cranking the film back a few feet and shooting the start of the new scene over the ending of the old. This device, known as the "dissolve," was quickly accepted by audiences as a movie convention, one that persists to this day.

The films of Georges Méliès—witty, inventive, filled with exuberant activity and fantastic imagination—were widely seen in this country through the first decade of the new century, and played an important part in convincing American producers that pictures could and should be longer than the conventional fifty feet (about one minute on the screen). Unfortunately, such showings were rarely to Méliès's financial advantage. In those days films were not rented but sold outright by the foot. Anyone with a print, of course, could strike off a new negative for a few dollars and sell "dupe" prints at far less than the original producer could afford. This practice, known as "pirating," persisted until authorized film rental exchanges were set up—but by that time Méliès had been driven out of business. He was found, years later, tending a news-stand in the Paris Métro, and died in 1938 in a home for destitute actors.

The sharp business practices of the era, however, were not the sole cause of Méliès's failure. In 1903 a film appeared that was to revolutionize all movie making, breaking decisively with stage forms and stage techniques and pointing toward a genuinely filmic style. *The Great Train Robbery by* Edwin S. Porter, one of America's pioneer director-photographers, revealed for the first time the function and the power of the cut in telling a story on the screen. Closely related to the chases and gun fights of the touring "Wild West" shows at the turn of the century, it tells of a mail train holdup by armed desperadoes, the formation of a posse and the pursuit and annihilation of the gunmen—all in about eight minutes of film. Each scene, taken from a single camera position, is complete in itself and advances the action one step further. Once a scene has been completed, however, Porter makes a flat cut to the next shot without titles, without dissolves or anything but the logic of the story to bridge the gap. Nor does the sequence of his scenes necessarily follow in strict chronological progression, as it had in all films up to that time. We see the robbers enter the station, bind and gag the telegraph operator, then steal aboard the train, all in proper sequence. But after they have held up the train and made their getaway, Porter switches back to the unfortunate operator just as he is discovered by his little daughter at the station. The two lines of action are taking place simultaneously—the robbers escaping, their crime discovered. Porter, boldly juggling with time, here demonstrated the possibilities of parallel editing, the concept that D.W. Griffith was to develop so dramatically a few years later. At another point, the action seems to leapfrog, jumping from the holdup on the train to the formation of the posse and then back to the gang making its escape. Again the scenes are given meaning and coherence by the editing process, the cutting that brings them together and relates them one to the other. In short, the technique that Porter had hit upon in assembling this unpretentious little Western provided the key to the whole art of film editing, the joining together of bits of film shot in different places and at different times to form a single, unified narrative.

VICTORY AGAINST RUSSIA CONFIRMS JAPAN'S GREAT POWER STATUS

SUISHENG ZHAO

After Japan was forcibly opened to Western trade and influence in the 1850s it modernized quickly, developing both an industrial economy and a military built along the lines of those of Britain and Germany. By the 1890s Japanese leaders felt ready to compete internationally. A successful war against China in 1895 gave Japan a sphere of interest in northern China, where the Russian empire also sought to assert its claims to territory and natural resources.

In the following selection, Suisheng Zhao examines the significance of the Russo-Japanese War, fought in 1904–1905. The war was a resounding military success for the Japanese, who sank virtually the entire Russian fleet. Zhao claims that Japan enjoyed the tacit support of the United States, which hoped to expand its own influence in Asia and acted aggressively to arrange a peace between Russia and Japan. Japan's victory marked, Zhao asserts, a turning point in world history: An East Asian power showed itself capable of competing on the international scene and, in the process, demonstrated to colonized peoples the world over that Europe's domination of the globe might be only temporary.

Suisheng Zhao is professor of government and East Asian politics at Colby College in Maine.

Excerpted from *Power Competition in East Asia: From the Old Chinese World Order to Post–Cold War Regional Multipolarity,* by Suisheng Zhao. Copyright © Suisheng Zhao. Reprinted with permission of St. Martin's Press, LLC.

The Russo-Japanese War was an event of the first magnitude for Japan, a veritable life-and-death struggle for the small island nation pitted against a European power. However, Japan had the advantage of fighting close to its main sources of supply. With control of the sea, the Japanese quickly landed troops on Port Arthur [Russia's main Pacific Ocean port]. There Japanese generals threw wave after wave of troops against entrenched machine gun positions in a lesson that seemingly went unnoticed by generals on the European continent until a decade later. After spectacular losses, Japanese forces prevailed. Later on, Shenyang (Mukden) fell in a collision of armies numbering 300,000 on each side. In the meantime, Russia's Baltic fleet was making its way painfully around the world after having its use of the Suez Canal denied by Japan's new ally, Great Britain. Immediately on its arrival in the Tsushima Straits, which separate Japan from Korea, the Russians found Japan's warships lying in wait. The Russian fleet was utterly demolished.

THE AMERICAN PRESIDENT BROKERS A PEACE

Despite military success, Japan responded favorably to the initiative taken by President Theodore Roosevelt of the United States to act as a peacemaker. The United States, while officially neutral during the war, was in reality a spiritual ally of Japan. Theodore Roosevelt was particularly fearful that Russian possession of Manchuria would be the beginning of a systematic effort to limit American commercial enterprise in northeast Asia. When the United States asked China to open three Manchurian cities—Tatongkou, Shenyang (Mukden), and Harbin—to foreign trade and to block Russia's exclusive privilege there, China under Russian pressure refused. Americans interpreted the Russian policy as a violation of the principle of the Open Door policy. Thus President Roosevelt thought that Japan was "playing our game" in the war against Russia. On the other hand, the president also realized that Japan might cause trouble to American possession in the Pacific and the Far East. Therefore, upon receiving Russian willingness to conclude a treaty of peace with Japan, and, in the meantime, receiving Japanese assurance that Japan would abide by the Open Door doctrine in Manchuria, would recognize Chinese sovereignty in the returned area, and would not harbor any aggressive design on the Philippines, President Roosevelt was able to bring the two warring nations around the conference table in Portsmouth [Rhode Island] in August 1905. With the Treaty of Portsmouth mediated by the United States on September 5, 1905, Japan obtained from Russia recognition of its paramount economic, political, and military interest in Korea, and special interests in Manchuria by possession of the Changchun-Dalian portion of the Russian-controlled Chinese Eastern Railway and the transfer from Russia of the Liaodong Peninsula. In order to protect these newly acquired rights, a Kanto (East Manchuria) army was created, which became the symbol of Japan's continental imperialism.

Japan's emergence as an expansionist power was an unbroken chain of events stretching from the Japanese opening of Korea in 1874 to the Sino-Japanese War in 1895 to the Russo-Japanese War in 1905. The victory over Russia had special historical significance because it was the first victory of an Asian nation over a major European power. It established Japan as the peer of the other Western Great Powers. If the Sino-Japanese War was a turning point that acquired for Japan its first overseas colonial possession (Taiwan), the Russo-Japanese War marked "the takeoff point of Japanese imperialism" due to "the establishment of a sphere of influence recognized by the other powers." The Russo-Japanese War established Japan's undisputed position among the foremost powers in East Asia. The result of the war diminished Russia's influence and opened a new chapter in world history. By demonstrating her national strength, Japan ushered in a new age of equal relations with the Western powers and secured formal recognition of its new sphere of influence by a series of bilateral agreements with Russia, Great Britain, the United States, and France. [As historian Peter Duus claimed,] "Western assent to the new Japanese position on the Asian mainland reflected a mixture of self-interest, indifference, and helplessness."

AN ABORTED REVOLUTION IN RUSSIA

LIONEL KOCHAN AND RICHARD ABRAHAM

Although Russia was a major military and imperial power, it remained backward by western Europe standards at the turn of the twentieth century. Its czar, Nicholas II, still ruled as an absolute monarch and a small nobility controlled the land and the army. Moreover, Russia had failed to industrialize, containing few large cities and only a very small educated middle class. Perhaps in response, Russian radicals were both more outspoken and more desperate than dissidents in other nations.

In the following selection, Lionel Kochan and Richard Abraham describe Russia's 1905 revolution, which broke out as Russia suffered a humiliating loss in the Russo-Japanese War. The authors claim that the revolution, which failed to produce any lasting political or social change, had two important effects. The first was to harden the stance of Russia's conservatives. The second was the formation of the St. Petersburg Soviet, a workers' and soldiers' council in the nation's most Westernized city. Such "soviets," although they were soon declared illegal, provided a forum for Russia's voiceless millions and a hope for radical leaders.

Lionel Kochan was professor of history at Warwick University in the United Kingdom. Richard Abraham is a headmaster at Battersea Council School in London.

Excerpted from *The Making of Modern Russia*, 2nd ed., by Lionel Kochan and Richard Abraham (Penguin Books, 1962, 1983). Copyright © Lionel Kochan, 1962. Copyright © Lionel Kochan and Richard Abraham, 1983. Reproduced by permission of Penguin Books, Ltd.

The sparks came on 22 January 1905. Port Arthur had fallen a few weeks earlier, the latest and the most crushing of a series of Russian defeats in the Far East. At much the same time a strike broke out in St Petersburg at the Putilov engineering works. It rapidly spread to other factories. Here, overnight almost, was a mass workers' movement of unprecedented dimensions. The tension rose to such a pitch that it forced a certain Father George Gapon, who led a police-sponsored labour union, either to take some positive action or to abdicate entirely and leave his members to follow an even more radical path. Gapon, in collaboration with some of the zemstvo [local government] leaders, intelligentsia, and Socialist-Revolutionaries, drafted a petition for presentation to the Tsar. It was couched for the most part in plaintive terms—'we are not considered human beings . . . we are treated like slaves'. But it also contained outspoken political demands: freedom of the Press, religion, assembly; the calling of a constituent assembly; equality before the law; labour legislation and the eight-hour day; a reduction in indirect taxes and the introduction of a graduated income tax; an amnesty for political prisoners; and an end to the war. One hundred and thirty-five thousand people signed the petition.

BLOODY SUNDAY

And so, on Sunday 22 January, about 150,000 people marched under Father Gapon's leadership, in a series of columns from the various suburbs to the Winter Palace. They were peaceful processions. The marchers intoned hymns, and bore icons and portraits of the Tsar [Nicholas II]. What followed was not only a crime but a political error of colossal dimensions. The military authorities were under instructions to accept no petitions (the Tsar was not in residence in the capital) but to disperse the crowds by whatever means proved necessary. In a series of incidents, the marching columns peacefully singing their hymns were met by stentorian commands to disperse which could not possibly be carried out quickly. Salvo after salvo poured into the terror-stricken marchers. At the end of 'Bloody Sunday' there were perhaps a thousand dead and many more thousands wounded. The Tsar's pitiful gesture in inviting a group of workers to share tea and cakes with him some weeks later failed to efface the reputation he now acquired as 'Bloody Nicholas'.

This was the spark that set alight the flame of revolution. In all social groups, in all parts of the country, revolt flared up. By the end of January nearly half a million workmen were on strike. The professional intelligentsia joined in. Doctors, lawyers, teachers, professors, engineers, formed unions to press political claims on the government. The terrorist movement flared up with the killing of the Tsar's uncle, the Grand Duke Sergei, who had made himself infamous for his cruelty during his Governor-Generalship of Moscow. Industrialists also joined in the clamour for a constitutional regime. A new feature of the popular movement was the formation of an All-Russian Peasants' Union—the first time that a political organization open to peasants had arisen on Russian soil. It soon joined the Union of Unions, led by the liberal leader Milyukov. In many parts of the country a state of anarchy prevailed that all the Tsar's courts martial and repression could not repress.

The Tsar, meanwhile, was hoping for military victories that would re-establish his shattered prestige and allow him to recall the armies from Manchuria. There came, instead, defeat at Mukden in Manchuria, and the destruction of the Russian Baltic Fleet at Tsushima in May 1905. The epic voyage of Rozhdestvensky's fleet halfway round the world to tip the balance of forces in the Far East had ended in total disaster. In a sense this was the end of one of the dreams of Peter the Great. No Russian fleet has fought a battle on the high seas since. In August, the Tsar bowed to the mounting pressure by issuing a law promising a consultative assembly, to be known as the Duma, to be formed from an electoral body weighted in favour of high property qualifications and also the peasantry. But this succeeded in splitting off only the wealthier and more right-wing liberals. To the rest of the population it was a matter for derision and boycott. To the workers, the proposed Duma meant nothing. They would have no vote in it at all.

A Workers' and Soldiers' Revolt

In the spring the first wave of strikes petered out, and the initiative passed to the middle classes. But in the summer and autumn the workers' movement suddenly revived. Not that the summer had seen any real break in the movement: troops had been called out in Lodz, and in the Black Sea fleet the crew of the battleship *Potyomkin* had mutinied—the subject of one of [Russian director Sergey] Eisenstein's most famous films. Also, of course, there were few provinces, especially in the border regions, where the peasants were not plundering the manors, despoiling the landowners' estates, raiding store-houses, burning land registers.

The events of the autumn eclipsed even these. In the second half of September, a printers' strike in St Petersburg touched off, with unexampled rapidity, what was in all but name a general strike. It came so swiftly and so spontaneously that even the revolutionaries were taken by surprise—as indeed they had been by most of the events of the year. Barricades sprang up on the streets of Odessa, Kharkov, Ekaterinoslav. The whole life of the country was paralysed. There were further mutinies among the troops. The countryside was ablaze with peasant violence. The climax came, both from the government's standpoint and that of the revolutionaries, in the middle of October. In view of the mounting chaos and the inability of the military hard-liners to guarantee a speedy return to order, Nicholas II was persuaded to issue a manifesto promising civil liberties and some sort of constitutional order and to appoint Witte [a modernizing aristocrat] as Russia's first Prime Minister. Simultaneously, he called on loyal Russians to rally round the throne; sure enough, riots broke out in which Jews and socialists were killed. At the same time, a new instrument of revolutionary democracy, the St Petersburg Soviet, emerged. These phenomena towered above the chaos and tumult of the year.

The October manifesto proclaimed fundamental civil liberties, promised to extend the franchise beyond the limits announced in July, and promised also that no law would be promulgated without the approval of the State Duma. Witte's premiership lasted just six months. During that time, he presided over Russia's first nation-wide elections, prepared a major peasant reform and negotiated a massive loan with foreign bankers that enabled the Tsar to dispense with both him and the Duma. Yet Witte's experiment was a failure. No part of the opposition would openly side with a government which continued to employ the military reactionaries to suppress the revolution. For his part, Nicholas II loathed and hated Witte for divesting him of some of his inherited prerogatives—particularly when he failed to restore order.

A Preview of 1917's Communist Revolution

The St Petersburg Soviet, formed of some 500 delegates elected by about 200,000 workers, represented the peak of working-class achievement. It has been called a spontaneous creation; this just means that its creators were neither famous themselves, nor operating under the instructions of the organizations of the revolutionary intelligentsia. But it was a lesson in revolution, not the revolution itself—the manifestation of the class autonomy urged by Plekhanov [an early Marxist thinker], not the revolutionary instrument of class power for which Lenin [a Marxist leader] was hoping. The Soviet, of which Trotsky [another important Marxist] became co-chairman, followed on the whole a moderate policy. It supported the general strike, but sought rather to educate the workers in the limitations of the Duma than to organize an immediate armed insurrection. 'A constitution is given, but the autocracy remains', said Trotsky. The most revolutionary act of the Soviet was to issue an appeal for the non-payment of taxes and the withdrawal of bank deposits.

Whatever they might think of the government, the liberal members of the middle classes were appalled by the emergence of the Soviet and even more by the revolts occurring throughout the country. The government, despite its own inner tensions and low morale, could proceed with the repression of the revolution. The leaders of the St Petersburg Soviet were arrested and an armed uprising in Moscow put down with relative ease. But even at the end of the year, with mutinies in the Sevastopol fleet, and revolts in Siberia, Batum, and Kharkov, it might seem that a renewed upsurge was in the making. In actual fact, the autumn had seen the climax. Not for more than a decade would it be overtopped by a second and even more tumultuous upheaval. One thing was clear: there would be no western-style bourgeois revolution in Russia. At the first sign of independent activity by the lower orders, the Russian bourgeoisie had dissociated itself from the revolution. The peasantry, on the other hand, would go on fighting for months and months after the workers had been put down. The Menshevik [of moderate, gradual reform] view of Russia's future development had been struck a blow from which it never fully recovered.

THREE MAJOR CHALLENGES TO EUROPE'S BALANCE OF POWER

WINSTON S. CHURCHILL

Since the downfall of Napoléon Bonaparte in 1815, European powers had enjoyed a rough balance of power that prevented major wars. The balance survived both the unifications of Italy and Germany and the rapid chase for international empires. A number of events occurred after 1900, however, that were to threaten the balance. Among them were the events described by Winston S. Churchill in the following selection: the first Moroccan crisis of 1905, a Balkan crisis in 1908, and Germany's rapid naval buildup.

The Moroccan crisis had the effect, Churchill asserts, of drawing France and the previously isolationist Britain closer together as well as demonstrating Germany's readiness to go to war with France. The Balkan crisis made apparent Germany's willingness to support Austria's territorial ambitions. Finally Churchill, who served as Britain's lord of the admiralty from 1911 to 1915, expressed great concern that Germany's growing navy could only be directed at challenging Britain. With hindsight, these events contributed to the outbreak of World War I in 1914.

Winston S. Churchill, in addition to serving as Britain's prime minister during World War II after a long political career, is the author of many works of history.

Excerpted from *The World Crisis, 1911–1914*, by Winston S. Churchill (London: Thornton Butterworth, 1923).

E arly in 1905 a French mission arrived in Fez. Their language and actions seemed to show an intention of treating Morocco as a French Protectorate. The Sultan of Morocco appealed to Germany, asking if France was authorized to speak in the name of Europe. Germany was now enabled to advance as the champion of an international agreement, which she suggested France was violating. Behind this lay the clear intention to show France that she could not afford in consequence of her agreement with Britain, to offend Germany. The action taken was of the most drastic character. The German Emperor was persuaded to go to Tangiers, and there, against his better judgment, on March 31, 1905, he delivered, in very uncompromising language chosen by his ministers, an open challenge to France. To this speech the widest circulation was given by the German Foreign Office. Hotfoot upon it (April 11 and 12) two very threatening despatches were sent to Paris and London, demanding a conference of all the Signatory Powers to the Treaty of Madrid [which pledged support for Moroccan autonomy in 1880]. Every means was used by Germany to make France understand that if she refused the conference there would be war; and to make assurance doubly sure a special envoy was sent from Berlin to Paris for that express purpose. . . .

So far Germany had been very successful. Under a direct threat of war she had compelled France to bow to her will, and to sacrifice the Minister who had negotiated the Agreement with Great Britain. [French premier] Rouvier's Cabinet sought earnestly for some friendly solution which, while sparing France the humiliation of a conference dictated in such circumstances, would secure substantial concessions to Germany. The German Government were, however, determined to exploit their victory to the full, and not to make the situation easier for France either before or during the conference. The conference accordingly assembled at Algeciras [in Spain] in January, 1906.

FRANCE AND BRITAIN UNITE AGAINST A GERMAN THREAT

Great Britain now appeared on the scene, apparently quite unchanged and unperturbed by her domestic convulsions. She had in no way encouraged France to refuse the conference. But if a war was to be fastened on France by Germany as the direct result of an agreement made recently in the full light of day between France and Great Britain, it was held that Great Britain could not remain indifferent. [Prime Minister] Sir Henry Campbell-Bannerman therefore authorized [Foreign Minister] Sir Edward Grey to support France strongly at Algeciras. He also authorized, almost as the first act of what was to be an era of Peace, Retrenchment, and Reform, the beginning of military conversations between the British and French General Staffs with a view to concerted action in the event of war. This was a step of profound significance and of far-reaching reactions. Henceforward the relations of the two Staffs became increasingly intimate and confidential. The minds of our military men were definitely turned into a particular channel. Mutual trust grew continually in one set of military relationships, mutual precautions in the other. However explicitly the two Governments might agree and affirm to each other that no national or political engagement was involved in these technical discussions, the fact remained that they constituted an exceedingly potent tie.

The attitude of Great Britain at Algeciras turned the scale against Germany. Russia, Spain and other signatory Powers associated themselves with France and England. Austria revealed to Germany the limits beyond which she would not go. Thus Germany found herself isolated, and what she had gained by her threats of war evaporated at the Council Board. In the end a compromise suggested by Austria, enabled Germany to withdraw without open loss of dignity. From these events, however, serious consequences flowed. Both the two systems into which Europe was divided, were crystallized and consolidated. Germany felt the need of binding Austria more closely to her. Her open attempt to terrorize France had produced a deep impression upon French public opinion. An immediate and thorough reform of the French Army was carried out, and the *Entente* with England was strengthened and confirmed. Algeciras was a milestone on the road to Armageddon. . . .

TROUBLE IN THE BALKANS

It was not long before the next European crisis arrived. On October 5, 1908, Austria, without warning or parley, proclaimed the annexation of Bosnia and Herzegovina. These provinces of the Turkish Empire had been administered by her under the Treaty of Berlin, 1878; and the annexation only declared in form what already existed in fact. The Young Turk Revolution which had occurred in the summer, seemed to Austria likely to lead to a reassertion of Turkish sovereignty over Bosnia and Herzegovina, and this she was concerned to forestall. A reasonable and patient diplomacy would probably have secured for Austria the easements which she needed. Indeed, negotiations with Russia, the Great Power most interested, had made favourable progress. But suddenly and abruptly Count Aerenthal, the Austrian Foreign Minister, interrupted the discussions, by the announcement of the

annexation, before the arrangements for a suitable concession
to Russia had been concluded.
By this essentially violent act a
public affront was put upon
Russia, and a personal slight
upon the Russian negotiator,
Monsieur Isvolsky.

A storm of anger and protest
arose on all sides. England, bas-
ing herself on the words of the
London Conference in 1871,
'That it is an essential principle of
the law of nations that no Power
can free itself from the engage-
ments of a Treaty, nor modify its
stipulations except by consent of
the contracting parties,' refused
to recognize either the annexation of Bosnia and Herzegovina

Winston S. Churchill

or the declaration of Bulgarian independence which had synchro-
nized with it. Turkey protested loudly against a lawless act. An effective boycott of Austrian merchandise was organized by the
Turkish Government. The Serbians mobilized their army. But it
was the effect on Russia which was most serious. The bitter ani-
mosity excited against Austria throughout Russia became a penul-
timate cause of the Great War. In this national quarrel the personal
differences of Aerenthal and Isvolsky played also their part.

Great Britain and Russia now demanded a conference, declin-
ing meanwhile to countenance what had been done. Austria,
supported by Germany, refused. The danger of some violent action on the part of Serbia became acute. Sir Edward Grey, after
making it clear that Great Britain would not be drawn into a war
on a Balkan quarrel, laboured to restrain Serbia, to pacify Turkey,
and to give full diplomatic support to Russia. The controversy
dragged on till April, 1909, when it was ended in the following
remarkable manner. The Austrians had determined, unless Serbia recognized the annexation of Bosnia and Herzegovina, to
send an ultimatum and to declare war upon her. At this point the
German Chancellor, Prince von Bülow, intervened. Russia, he insisted, should herself advise Serbia to give way. The Powers
should officially recognize the annexation without a conference
being summoned and without any kind of compensation to Serbia. Russia was to give her consent to this action, without previously informing the British or French Governments. If Russia did

not consent, Austria would declare war on Serbia *with the full and complete support of Germany*. Russia, thus nakedly confronted by war both with Austria and Germany, collapsed under the threat, as France had done three years before. England was left an isolated defender of the sanctity of Treaties and the law of nations. The Teutonic triumph was complete. But it was a victory gained at a perilous cost. France, after her treatment in 1905, had begun a thorough military reorganization. Now Russia, in 1910, made an enormous increase in her already vast army; and both Russia and France, smarting under similar experiences, closed their ranks, cemented their alliance, and set to work to construct with Russian labour and French money the new strategic railway systems of which Russia's western frontier stood in need. . . .

GERMANY CHALLENGES BRITISH CONTROL OF THE SEAS

It was next the turn of Great Britain to feel the pressure of the German power.

In the spring of 1909, the First Lord of the Admiralty, Mr. McKenna, suddenly demanded the construction of no less than six Dreadnought battleships. He based this claim on the rapid growth of the German Fleet and its expansion and acceleration under the new naval law of 1908, which was causing the Admiralty the greatest anxiety. I was still a sceptic about the danger of the European situation, and not convinced by the Admiralty case. In conjunction with the Chancellor of the Exchequer, I proceeded at once to canvass this scheme and to examine the reasons by which it was supported. The conclusions which we both reached were that a programme of four ships would sufficiently meet our needs. In this process I was led to analyse minutely the character and composition of the British and German Navies, actual and prospective. I could not agree with the Admiralty contention that a dangerous situation would be reached in the year 1912. I found the Admiralty figures on this subject were exaggerated. I did not believe that the Germans were building Dreadnoughts secretly in excess of their published Fleet Laws. I held that our margin in pre-Dreadnought ships would, added to a new programme of four Dreadnoughts, assure us an adequate superiority in 1912, 'the danger year' as it was then called. In any case, as the Admiralty only claimed to lay down the fifth and sixth ships in the last month of the financial year, i.e. March, 1910, these could not affect the calculations. The Chancellor of the Exchequer and I therefore proposed that four ships should be sanctioned for 1909, and that the additional two should be considered in relation to the programme of 1910. . . .

Whatever differences might be entertained about the exact number of ships required in a particular year, the British nation in general became conscious of the undoubted fact that Germany proposed to reinforce her unequalled army by a navy which in 1920 would be far stronger than anything up to the present possessed by Great Britain. To the Navy Law of 1900 had succeeded the amending measure of 1906; and upon the increases of 1906 had followed those of 1908. In a flamboyant speech at Reval in 1904 the German Emperor had already styled himself 'The Admiral of the Atlantic.' All sorts of sober-minded people in England began to be profoundly disquieted. What did Germany want this great navy for? Against whom, except us, could she measure it, match it, or use it? There was a deep and growing feeling, no longer confined to political and diplomatic circles, that the Prussians meant mischief, that they envied the splendour of the British Empire, and that if they saw a good chance at our expense, they would take full advantage of it. Moreover, it began to be realized that it was no use trying to turn Germany from her course by abstaining from counter measures. Reluctance on our part to build ships was attributed in Germany to want of national spirit, and as another proof that the virile race should advance to replace the effete over-civilized and pacifist society which was no longer capable of sustaining its great place in the world's affairs. No one could run his eyes down the series of figures of British and German construction for the first three years of the Liberal Administration, without feeling in presence of a dangerous, if not a malignant, design.

In 1905 Britain built 4 ships, and Germany 2.

In 1906 Britain *decreased* her programme to 3 ships, and Germany *increased* her programme to 3 ships.

In 1907 Britain *further decreased* her programme to 2 ships, and Germany *further increased* her programme to 4 ships.

These figures are monumental.

It was impossible to resist the conclusion, gradually forced on nearly everyone, that if the British Navy lagged behind, the gap would be very speedily filled.

THE CHINESE REVOLUTION ENDS 2000 YEARS OF DYNASTIC TRADITION

SUN YAT-SEN

In 1911 Chinese revolutionaries, frustrated by both the corrupt and incompetent Ching dynasty and China's increasing subjection to Western powers, overthrew the Ching emperor and proclaimed China a republic. For the first time in over two thousand years China would not be governed by a family dynasty of absolute emperors.

The new republic elected as its first leader Sun Yat-sen, who was educated in Hawaii and British Hong Kong. He ruled only briefly but reemerged to become the leader of China's republican party, the Kuomintang. The following selection is from Sun Yat-sen's memoirs, published in 1918. Sun Yat-sen recognizes that China's civilization was ancient, proud, and very capable. But he asserts that China has grown complacent and failed to learn from the West and turn those lessons to China's advantage.

C hina is one of the oldest states in the world. Her culture has five thousand years behind it, and, before relations with foreign Powers began, it occupied the first place amongst the Oriental states. The invasion of foreign tribes could not wipe out Chinese customs and ritual. The neighbouring States either expressed their allegiance to China, or sought her

Excerpted from *Memoirs of a Chinese Revolutionary*, by Sun Yat-sen, (Taipei: China Cultural Service, 1918).

friendship and borrowed Chinese culture. But owing to the fact that China became the leading State, and that the Chinese had before their eyes no example of another state equal to her, conceit, self-satisfaction and arrogance arose. All this entered into our flesh and blood, and we were transformed into a nation apart. We were our own teachers, as in all reconstruction we made use only of our own resources and strength, without resorting to foreign help.

When a solitary individual is wrecked on a desert island, he has to procure for himself all he requires. He ploughs himself, and consumes as food the fruits of the soil. He spins himself, and wears the yarn he spins, etc. Altogether he carries out the most varied processes of production, and being overloaded with work is unable to commune with his own thoughts. He loses all sense of the meaning of social co-operation. When, in the course of time and for various reasons, this desert island turns out to be on a world shipping route, and it is visited by foreign merchants, they will note the irksome toil of this man and say: "My dear sir, it is quite unnecessary for you to do everything at once, it would be sufficient if you concentrated on one kind of production. This would economise your time and make you master of your own labour." The man, undoubtedly, will not believe them at once, because his state of development will not permit him to do so. He will consider it impossible. The Chinese at the present time in the same way will not believe that China can at one jump raise herself to a high level of power and well-being.

CHINA FAILS TO LEARN FROM OTHERS

Therefore the self-centredness of China and her conceited self-satisfaction have been noted of old. The majority of Chinese cannot understand the benefits of international co-operation, and therefore will not tolerate the thought of any superiority over themselves, or of allowing others to correct their mistakes. This has made China narrow-minded, and undoubtedly has hindered her progress.

Over sixty or seventy years have passed since foreign Powers broke down the Great Wall and came into China, yet Chinese thought still remains that of a solitary man thrown on a desert island. Therefore China is still unable to utilise foreign knowledge and resources to strengthen her own power as a nation.

China as a State possesses colossal territories, incalculable wealth, vast quantities of human energy, and in spite of all resembles a rich old man, who possesses extensive parks, lands and treasures, with a large family, but incapable of keeping house. The lands are deserted and overgrown with weeds, the treasures are kept under lock and key and left without use, while the children and grandchildren are idle, and hunger and cold reign in the house. The house of such an old man gives us the picture of China to-day.

My fellow-countrymen know that our country is moving towards destruction. And if even the animals have a sense of duty to their family and home, man must, without doubt, inwardly feel his duty to help his country. The citizens of China, who not only inhabit our country, but strive that it may be great and flourish, have many ways of bringing this about.

REVOLUTIONARY UPHEAVAL IN MEXICO

Martin Luis Guzman

In the following selection, Martin Luis Guzman describes the events of the Mexican Revolution in 1911. The revolution developed after the long-term president of Mexico, the dictator Porfirio Díaz, unexpectedly lost an election. Many voters wanted a more progressive candidate who supported reforms such as freer trade and greater protection of individual rights. This election led to nearly a decade of instability throughout Mexico.

According to Guzman, the source of much of this instability was a suppressed desire among many people for justice and national revival. Their opportunity arose when Díaz's presidential successor, Francisco Madero, in whom reformers had placed their faith, was assassinated by the army. Leaders arose to challenge the conservative forces such as military leaders sympathetic to Díaz. Guzman goes on to suggest that revolutionary leaders, however, lacked common goals, and that their efforts at reform soon became a mere struggle for power.

Born in Mexico in 1887, Martin Luis Guzman worked as a journalist before joining the forces of guerrilla leader Pancho Villa in the early years of the Mexican Revolution.

I n 1910 Porfirio Díaz's dictatorship was still supreme—a liberal, progressive dictatorship. That same year, as the time for presidential elections approached—a periodical farce by which the letter of the Constitution was observed—the nation began to give evident signs that it wanted to regain possession of its civic will, which had been lost since 1880. In opposition to the

Excerpted from the Foreword to *The Eagle and the Serpent*, by Martin Luis Guzman (Gloucester, MA: Peter Smith Publisher, 1969). Reprinted with permission of the publisher.

invariable candidacy of Díaz, which satisfied only the groups in power, the nation put forward another, that of Francisco I. Madero. The dictator, however, paid no attention to these premonitory indications; he and his supporters attempted to continue in power, whereupon Madero, at the head of a rising which was not merely political, but revolutionary in character, overthrew Porfirio Díaz and took over the presidency after new elections held in 1911.

A PRESIDENTIAL ASSASSINATION

Madero was a reformer of gentle, apostolic character. He preached ideals of justice and a faith in the triumph of the right. As head of the government he attempted to divert the revolutionary tendencies he headed into legal channels. He also decided, in order to preserve the material well-being of the country, not to destroy the administrative machinery or the political instruments created by the dictatorship. He maintained the existing army; he respected the courts and the legislative bodies and made no changes in the personnel of the government departments. And in this way he lost the sympathy and support of his friends and delivered himself into the hands of his enemies, with results that were soon to prove fatal. A part of the army, headed by two ambitious generals, Bernardo Reyes and Felix Díaz, rose in February, 1913; another division, under the command of Victoriano Huerta, revolted a few days later, after solemnly swearing its loyalty. And then, all joining forces, Huerta had the revolutionary President assassinated a few hours after usurping his office.

The indignation and anger of the populace were so great that the day after Madero's death the real revolution broke out; the ideals of justice and agrarian reform the "martyr President" had advocated seemed too conservative; a vehement desire to regenerate everything asserted itself, an impulse to transform the whole social fabric of Mexico in its diverse aspects; and before the end of February the conflict had been kindled again. Venustiano Carranza, the governor of Coahuila, a civilian, was named First Chief of the revolutionary army; the political purposes of the new uprising were outlined in the Plan of Guadalupe, drawn up on March 27, 1913.

This new phase of the Revolution was much more widespread than the first. From the beginning there were four principal centers of revolutionary action, three in the north: Sonora, Chihuahua, and Coahuila; and one in the south: Morelos. The military leaders in the various sections of the north were respectively, Alvaro Obregón, Francisco Villa, and Pablo González; the leader in the south was Emiliano Zapata.

The advance of the four revolutionary armies, which was very slow at first, finally became irresistible, especially after the big battles won by Villa and Felipe Angeles in Torreón and Zacatecas. In the northwest, through the states of Sonora, Sinaloa, Nayarit and Jalisco, Obregón marched from victory to victory, all the way from the American border to the heart of Mexico. After Villa had broken through the main division of Huerta's army, Pablo González could move forward from the states of the northeast—that is to say, Tamaulipas, Nuevo León, and San Luis. And as Zapata was becoming more and more of a menace from the south—his activities had spread through the states of Morelos, Mexico, and Puebla, surrounding the capital—Huerta fled from the country seventeen months after his crime. After wiping out a part of Porfirio Díaz's former army and discharging from the service those who surrendered, the revolutionary troops marched into the city of Mexico in August 1914.

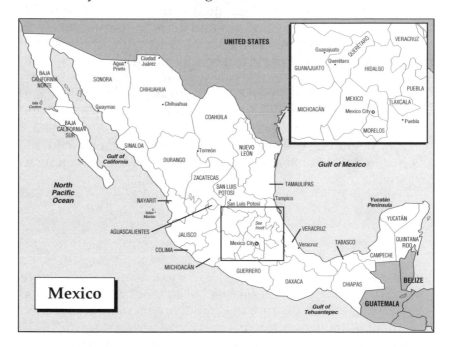

UNCERTAIN GOALS

But the Revolution was already divided in its hour of triumph. Carranza, whose background and formation were those of the dictatorship, and who was devoid of sincere and deep revolutionary ideals and eager only for power, from the first moment did all he could to bar the advancement of all those revolutionists whose independence or whose faith in the just character of the Revolution might prove a stumbling block to the new leaders in the race of their personal ambitions. He was supported in this by Obregón and by the groups of Sonora and Coahuila, and he even went so far as to put obstacles in the way of Villa's and Angeles's military operations. This lost him the support of many leaders and large sections of the country; and it brought about a wide breach, which was already evident in December 1913, and of a frankly hostile character by August 1914.

To put an end to these dissensions, which threatened to destroy the fruits of the Revolution's military victories, the leaders of the different groups decided to call an assembly which should have sovereign authority, to be composed of generals and governors. This was the Convention. It met in October 1914, first in Mexico City and then in Aguascalientes, and voted to remove both Carranza and Villa from their commands, as their quarrels were the principal cause of strife, and to name General Eulalio Gutiérrez president *pro tem* of the Republic. The generals and governors in favor of Villa submitted to the terms laid down by the Convention; but as Carranza and his adherents demanded, as a preliminary to their obedience of orders, the fulfillment of certain conditions that could not be accepted, the new President had to temporize with Villa while waiting for the Carranza faction to recognize his authority. Finally, disowned by the one and at the mercy of the other, he left the power in December 1914 and took refuge with his soldiers.

By the beginning of 1915 the Revolution had degenerated into a veritable state of anarchy, into a simple struggle between rivals for power.

WOMEN SEEKING THE RIGHT TO VOTE MUST REMAIN MILITANT

EMMELINE PANKHURST

The following selection is from a speech made in 1912 in London's Albert Hall by Emmeline Pankhurst. In 1903 Pankhurst founded, with her daughters Christabel and Sylvia, an organization known as the Women's Political and Social Union (WPSU). Their goal was to convince the Parliament of Great Britain to grant women the right to vote. Their efforts earned them the title of suffragettes, a word that many considered sarcastic and insulting since it implied that these women were behaving girlishly and did not need to be taken seriously.

In 1910 the WPSU grew militant, convinced that the government would not be swayed by argument alone. Members of the organization engaged in not only public demonstrations but also arson, window breaking, and sabotage. Arrested and jailed for her participation, Emmeline Pankhurst began a hunger strike, which British authorities countered by force-feeding her through a tube inserted down her throat. The force-feeding ruined Pankhurst's health and created greater sympathy for her cause.

In this portion of her speech, Pankhurst reminds women that they must remain militant in demanding their political rights, particularly in the face of such practices as prostitution, to which she refers as White Slave Traffic. Many people defended prostitution as a necessary outlet for the health of respectable families; Pankhurst saw it as an unnecessary evil that votes for women could remedy by elevating women's status and opportunity.

Excerpted from a speech given by Emmeline Pankhurst, London, 1912.

Now, why are we militant? There are women in this hall who still think it right to be patient, who still think they can afford to wait until there is time to deal with the enfranchisement of women. I tell you, women, in this hall that you who feel like that, you who allow yourselves to be tricked by the excuses of politicians, have not yet awakened to a realisation of the situation. The day after the outrages in Wales I met some of the women who had exposed themselves to the indecent assaults of that mob. I say "indecent" advisedly, because in addition to the facts reported in the newspapers—facts verified by photographs—in spite of the contradictions of Mr. Lloyd George [the Chancellor of the Exchange], in addition to what found its place in the newspapers, those women suffered from assaults of a kind which it was impossible to print in a decent newspapers. There was one woman whom I saw the day after, a woman with grown up children, the mother of a son twenty-five years of age. She described to me the way in which she had been assaulted. She said she did not feel she could even tell her husband or her son the nature of the assault, and then I said to her, "How could you bear it! It seems to me that is the hardest thing of all to bear." And she said, "All the time I thought of the women who day by day, and year by year, are suffering through the White Slave Traffic [prostitution] and I said to myself, "I will bear this, and even worse than this, to help to win power to put an end to that abominable slavery." In our speeches on Woman Suffrage, we have not dwelt very much on that horrible aspect of women's lives, because some of us felt that to think of those things, to speak very much about them, was apt to cause a state of feeling which would make it impossible for us to carry on our work with cheerful hearts, and with courage and with hope; but it seems to me that recent developments—legal developments—with regard to that question have made it essential that we should use that question to rouse women to a realisation of the simple fact that until women have the Vote, the White Slave Traffic will continue all over the world. Until by law we can establish an equal moral code for men and women, women will be fair game for the vicious section of the population inside Parliament as well as outside it.

SAFEGUARDING THE RIGHTS OF ALL WOMEN

Women will be fair game for the worst section of the population, inside Parliament as well as outside. People will tell you that in order that you may live happy and protected lives it is necessary. That is a lie. But even were it the horrible truth, there are other things we women have to deal with. Even if we tolerated the degradation of the grown women, can we tolerate the degrada-

Emmeline Pankhurst, founder of the Women's Political and Social Union, fought to grant women the right to vote and worked to elevate their social status.

tion of the helpless little children? When I began this militant campaign in the early days of the movement, I was a Poor Law Guardian, and it was my duty to go through the workhouse infirmary, and never shall I forget seeing a little girl of thirteen lying in bed, playing with a doll, and when I asked what was her illness I was told that she was on the eve of becoming a mother, and she was infected with a loathsome disease, and on the point of bringing, no doubt, a diseased child into the world. Wasn't that enough? A little later, in a by-election campaign against the

Government candidate in Leeds I had occasion to visit a Salvation Army hotel in that city, and in the matron's room there was a little child eleven years of age. She didn't look older than eight, and I said: "How was it she was there? Why wasn't she playing with other children?" And they said to me: "We dare not let her play with other children. She has been on the streets for more than a year." These, women in this meeting, are facts. These are not sensational stories taken from books written to attract the attention of those who like to think about matters that we have been accustomed to believe ought not to be spoken about. These I vouch for from my own experience, and they are but specimens and examples of a horrible state of things which flourishes in every so-called civilised centre of Europe and of the whole world.

THE SINKING OF THE TITANIC MARKS THE END OF AN ERA

WALTER LORD

At noon on April 12, 1912, the luxury liner R.M.S. *Titanic* departed Southampton, England, on its maiden voyage to New York City. It was the largest passenger ship ever built and a triumph of Western engineering, organization, and finance. Among its twenty-four hundred passengers and crew were a large number of the international elite of Europe and America, who were accustomed to frequent and luxurious transatlantic crossings. As Walter Lord writes in the following excerpt, the first years of the twentieth century offered this elite a life of unbelievable luxury and comfort. Taking advantage of the bounty of an industrial economy and the vast colonial empires of the age, the rich moved casually from fashionable resort to fashionable resort enjoying the latest pastimes and entertainments and flaunting their privileges in the faces of those poorer or darker-skinned than they.

On April 14, shortly before midnight, the *Titanic* struck an iceberg in the North Atlantic and sank, killing more than fifteen hundred of its passengers. As Lord suggests, when this greatest-ever ship sank, it took with it not only many of the bodies but also the confidence of Europe's and America's elites, who "never felt completely sure of anything again."

Walter Lord is the author of a number of histories including *A Night to Remember*, an account of the sinking of the *Titanic*.

Excerpted from *The Good Years: From 1900 to the First World War,* by Walter Lord. Copyright 1960 by Walter Lord. Reprinted by permission of Sterling Lord Literistic, Inc.

I n the past ten years [1902–1912] a large set of fashionable people had developed a pattern of life that went far beyond the boundaries of any one nation. Americans, British, and a sprinkling of [European] Continentals, they lived an international life of their own . . . restlessly migrating from country to country, from season to season. They were extravagant, frivolous, often foolish, but they were perhaps the most truly cosmopolitan group the world has ever seen.

The coronation [of Edward] was a natural rallying point, but this set needed no special event to get together. Even when nothing was happening, they made their rounds; and even when they didn't do anything, they still were news. "Mrs. Stuyvesant Fish has made no plans to spend the summer in Europe," the *New York Times* breathlessly announced as the 1911 season approached.

FROM RESORT TO SPA

Most of the group ran more true to form, and once the coronation was over resumed their regular orbit. In June it might be Newport, but more likely it was Paris, for it was already time for the racing at Longchamps.

In August, it was Cowes for the Regatta. Or perhaps Aix-les-Bains, or Lucerne, or the French channel resorts. In 1911 Dinard was especially popular, and here too the American influence was strong. Everyone danced the "Triple Boston," and all efforts failed to start something else . . . although not entirely due to the new step's beat. "An attempt was made this week to introduce the latest dance, The Tango," reported the *New York Times*; "after a few experiments, however, it was discarded, as the majority of dancers found it a little risque. . . ."

September found everyone "taking the cure" at Marienbad, Carlsbad, Homburg, and the other German baths. This was perhaps the most essential part of the whole routine, for at these resorts Society was literally flushed out and prepared for another year of Seasons. The "cure" could apparently do anything. According to an ad in the *Tribune,* Marienbad (Edward's favorite resort) was good for "Corpulence, gout, anemia, chronic appendicitis, constipation, arteriosclerosis, women's diseases, heart diseases, kidney trouble, nerves, etc."

Autumn was a time for Americans to return home. They entertained on weekends . . . served enormous breakfasts . . . played the new auction bridge . . . and when in town, caught up on the theatre. It was a miserable season on Broadway this fall, but those who suffered through *The Hen Pecks* at least discovered a thrilling new dancer named Vernon Castle.

New Year's, 1912, found the group on the go again. The restless Wideners and a few others gingerly nibbled at Palm Beach, but most fashionable Americans headed straight for the Riviera— Cannes, Nice, Menton, and above all, Monte Carlo. There they rejoined their English and Continental cohorts, who arrived on trains so luxurious that the passengers dressed for the dining car.

April, and the sun again touched Paris. One by one the great houses opened, and the usual round of salons and soirées began. The hotels were rapidly filling too, crowded with people returning from the south—Lord and Lady Decies at the Meurice . . . the John Jacob Astors at the Ritz. The Astors, however, would not stay long. One glance at the bride—or the proud, beaming colonel—quickly told why. "They will return to America," the *Times* coyly announced, "where an interesting event is likely to occur shortly."

PACKING FOR THE *TITANIC*

Mrs. Charlotte Drake Martinez Cardeza was another fashionable American heading back this April. In her case there was no impending "event," but she had been abroad ten months, and even the most inveterate members of the coterie liked to check home once in a while.

For Mrs. Cardeza this was no simple matter. Like the rest of the international set, she traveled with a fantastic amount of baggage. Every time she moved, fourteen trunks, four suitcases, three crates, and a medicine chest went along. Now it was time again. Once more her long-suffering maid packed the wardrobe that so accurately etched the world she knew—the latest creations from Worth . . . the blue satin tea gown from Ungar of Vienna . . . the white China silk waist from Carlsbad . . . the parasol from Lucerne . . . the ermine muff from Dresden . . . the baby lamb coat from St. Petersburg. It all added up to seventy dresses, ten fur coats, thirty-eight large feather pieces, twenty-two hat pins to keep them in place, ninety-one pairs of gloves, and innumerable trifles to amuse her, like the little Swiss music box in the shape of a bird.

Somehow it all was packed and loaded aboard the tender that bobbed out from Cherbourg in the early April twilight. Now as they chugged through the harbor, Mrs. Cardeza—like the Astors and everyone else there—must have felt the thrill that always comes with the start of an Atlantic voyage. No matter how often they did it—no matter how blasé they were about this endless round of Seasons—the ocean trip always seemed new and exciting. They felt it as they looked up from the tender at the forest of masts and funnels . . . the hundreds of portholes twinkling in the dusk . . . the bright ribbon of light that marked the promenade deck, lined with friends already on board.

And tonight there were many familiar faces in the crowd—people who had started earlier from Southampton. The George Wideners were there—they had gone to London for a suitable trousseau for their daughter Eleanor. So was Clarence Moore of Washington, who had been buying up English foxhounds for the Loudoun hunt . . . and Archie Butt, President Taft's stylish military aide.

The trip couldn't help but be fun, and all the more if you were young and attractive like Gretchen Longley of Hudson, New York, a pretty American student in Paris. In her little cabin she excitedly tore open a final bon voyage letter. It came from a friend left behind, who sent her a separate good wish for each day of the voyage:

> Good weather
> Refreshments (chocolate cakes)
> Every desire
> Tommies [lots of young men] to burn
> Chocolate ice-cream
> Heavenly evenings
> Entire meals
> No regrets.

There was no chance to get farther than "chocolate ice cream," for this was the *Titanic*, and on the fifth night out the great new "unsinkable" liner had a rendezvous with ice in the black, lonely waters of the North Atlantic. Two hours later—while her band played pleasant music on the sloping deck—she slipped beneath the sea. In this most unbelievable of disasters, over fifteen hundred people were lost—including the cream of a confident, complacent Society that never felt completely sure of anything again.

CHRONOLOGY

1842

Great Britain defeats China's Ching dynasty in the first Opium War. China is forced to open itself to widespread western trade and western influence as well as grant Britain a colony on Hong Kong Island.

1848

Gold is discovered at Sutter's Mill near Sacramento, California. By 1849 news of the discovery inspires people worldwide to join the California gold rush.

1848

The Taiping Rebellion in China begins. Rebels ultimately control vast territories in central China, but their rebellion is crushed by 1864.

1848

Unsuccessful revolutions throughout Europe call for the spread of liberal democracy and inspire Karl Marx and Friedrich Engels to publish *The Communist Manifesto*.

1851

Napoléon III, the great-nephew of Napoléon Bonaparte, becomes the emperor of France and puts his nation on the road to international imperialism.

1851

Britain stages the Great Exhibition at its Crystal Palace in London. The event, the first World's Fair, demonstrates Britain's predominance in technology, industry, and colonialism.

1853

American naval commander Commodore Matthew Perry brings a fleet of steam warships to the harbor of Tokyo, Japan. His goal, reached in 1854, is to force Japan's Tokugawa Shogunate to open their country to foreign trade and diplomacy.

1857

Indian soldiers in Great Britain's army in India rebel against their officers, seeking to throw the British out of India and revive the Mughal Empire. The event, the Sepoy Rebellion, is quelled with great violence by Britain.

1859

Charles Darwin publishes *On the Origin of Species*, his first description of his theory of natural selection.

1859

France begins the process of creating the colony of French Indochina, consisting of the modern nations of Vietnam, Laos, and Cambodia. The process is completed by 1893.

1861

America's Civil War begins.

1862

Napoléon III's France, with the support of Britain and Spain, invades Mexico. The European powers hope to forestall America's growing domination of the Western Hemisphere by installing a puppet emperor, Maximilian I, on Mexico's throne.

1864

Italy's unification, except for the city of Rome, is concluded.

1865

The Civil War in America ends with 600,000 deaths, territorial destruction, and the assassination of President Abraham Lincoln. Among the results is the freeing of millions of southern slaves.

1868

Japan's Meiji Restoration begins when the Tokugawa leaders are forced out by young men seeking to modernize the nation. During the Meiji period, which lasts until 1912, Japan rises to global power status.

1869

The Suez Canal connecting the Mediterranean Sea with the Red Sea and Indian Ocean is opened.

1871

After defeating Napoléon III's France in a brief war, Germany completes its unification. The German Empire becomes the dominant power on the European continent.

1872

Queen Victoria of Great Britain adds the title of Empress of India.

1876

Alexander Graham Bell invents the telephone.

1879

Thomas Edison perfects the incandescent electric light bulb. Soon after he opens his first electric power station in New York City.

1882

The scramble for Africa begins when King Leopold II of Belgium begins the creation of the Congo Free State, in effect a colony of Belgium. Over the next twenty years most of the remainder of the continent is divided up by the European colonial powers.

1882

The British army occupies Egypt to ensure British access to the Suez Canal.

1884

Germany's Iron Chancellor, Otto von Bismarck, calls together the Berlin Conference. His goal is to make sure the colonization of Africa proceeds peacefully.

1885

The Indian National Congress, which leads the struggle for the independence of India, is formed.

1885

The German inventor Karl Benz demonstrates a successful internal combustion engine.

1891

French automobile inventor Armand Peugeot drives his car over fifteen hundred miles without a problem.

1893

American businessmen take over the independent Kingdom of Hawaii and offer it to the American government.

1893

Thomas Edison opens the first film studio. It produces brief clips for vaudeville shows and peep-show parlors, or "nickelodeons."

1895

Italian engineer Guglielmo Marconi successfully transmits the first radio signals.

1895

Japan defeats China in the Sino-Japanese War, thereby establishing itself as a colonial power.

1896

Theodor Herzl, an Austrian journalist, launches the Zionist movement. His hope is to create a Jewish national state in Palestine.

1897

The British Empire celebrates the Diamond Anniversary of Queen Victoria's reign. The occasion also celebrates the British Empire, the largest ever created, which dominates one-quarter of the earth's land and people.

1898

Victory in the Spanish-American War gives the United States control of many of Spain's colonies, including Puerto Rico, Guam, and the Philippines.

1899

The Anglo-Boer War for control of South Africa begins. In 1902 it ends with a British victory.

1900

Sigmund Freud publishes *The Interpretation of Dreams*.

1900

The Boxer Rebellion in China attempts to toss out western imperialists. Although rebels enjoy the support of the Ching empress Cixi, the rebellion is crushed by a coalition of forces from Britain, France, Germany, Russia, Japan, and the United States.

1903

The Wright Brothers successfully fly an airplane at Kitty Hawk, North Carolina.

1903

Emmeline Pankhurst forms the Women's Social and Political Union in Great Britain. Her primary goal is to fight for women's suffrage.

1903

Robert Porter produces *A Great Train Robbery*, considered by many to be the first true motion picture.

1904

The Russo-Japanese War breaks out. It ends with a resounding Japanese victory, the first major victory of a non-Western over a Western power in many decades.

1905

An unsuccesful revolution takes place in Russia. It is inspired by Russia's continuing social conservatism as well as the hardships and humiliation brought about by the nation's defeat at the hands of Japan.

1905

The first Moroccan Crisis, reflecting the struggle between France and Germany over control of that North African country, nearly leads to European war.

1906

Britain launches its first dreadnought, a huge steam-powered warship. Germany soon matches it and pledges to surpass Britain in naval power.

1908

As the Turkish Empire loses influence in southeastern Europe, both Russia and the Austrian Empire seek to step into the void. Conflicts over influence in the Balkans nearly bring Europe to war as Germany sides with Austria.

1910

The Mexican Revolution begins.

1910

The women's suffrage movement in Britain turns militant, with "suffragettes" staging demonstrations, window-breaking campaigns, and other public disturbances.

1911

The second Moroccan Crisis again brings Europe to the brink of war.

1911

China's Ching dynasty is overthrown by forces hoping to turn China into a republic. Their leader, Sun Yat Sen, believes that China can learn, selectively, from the West.

1912

The *Titanic*, a product of the latest in Western engineering, organization, and finance, sinks after striking an iceberg.

1914

World War I begins. Britain's Foreign Secretary Edward Grey declares, "the lamps have gone out all over Europe. We will never see them lit again during our lifetime."

=| FOR FURTHER RESEARCH |=

Primary Sources

Chinua Achebe, *Things Fall Apart*. New York: Fawcett Crest, 1959.

A.A. Brill, ed. and trans., *The Basic Writings of Sigmund Freud*. New York: The Modern Library/Random House, 1938.

Winston S. Churchill, *The World Crisis 1911–1914*. London: Thornton Butterworth, 1923.

Joseph Conrad, *Heart of Darkness*. New York: Harper and Brothers, 1910.

Benedetto Croce, *History of Europe in the Nineteenth Century*. Trans. Henry Furst. New York: Harcourt, Brace, and World, 1933.

Charles Darwin, *On the Origin of Species*. Cambridge, MA: Harvard University Press, 1964.

Theodore S. Hamerow, ed., *The Age of Bismarck: Documents and Interpretations*. New York: Harper and Row, 1973.

Theodor Herzl, *Zionist Writings: Essays and Addresses*. Vol. 2. Trans. Harry Zohn. New York: Herzl Press, 1975.

Cheryl R. Jorgensen-Earp, ed., *Speeches and Trials of the Militant Suffragettes*. Madison, NJ: Fairleigh Dickinson University Press/Associated University Presses, 1999.

Rudyard Kipling, *Kim*. New York: Bantam Books, 1983.

Rudyard Kipling's Verse: Definitive Edition. Garden City, NY: Doubleday, 1940.

Henry Cabot Lodge, *The War with Spain*. New York: Harper and Brothers, 1899.

Karl Marx and Friedrich Engels, *The Communist Manifesto*. Trans. Samuel Moore. Harmondsworth, Middlesex, England: Penguin Books, 1967.

George Bernard Shaw, *Man and Superman*. New York: Airmont, 1965.

Sun Yat-sen, *Memoirs of a Chinese Revolutionary*. Taipei, Taiwan: China Cultural Service, 1953. (Originally published 1918).

Leo Tolstoy, *"Bethink Yourselves": Tolstoy's Letter on the Russian Japanese War*. Boston: American Peace Society, 1904.

European Society and Politics

Asa Briggs, *Victorian People*. New York: Harper and Row, 1963.

Lionel Kochan and Richard Abraham, *The Making of Modern Russia*. 2nd ed. Harmondsworth, Middlesex, England: Penguin Books, 1982.

Walter Lord, *The Good Years: From 1900 to the First World War*. New York, Harper and Brothers, 1960.

————, *A Night to Remember: The Sinking of the Titanic*. New York: Holt, 1955.

Antonia Raeburn, *The Militant Suffragettes*. London: Joseph, 1973.

Norman Rich, *The Age of Nationalism and Reform 1850–1890*. New York: Norton, 1977.

William L. Shirer, *The Rise and Fall of the Third Reich*. New York: Fawcett Crest, 1950.

Eugen Weber, *France: Fin de Siecle*. Cambridge, MA: Belknap Press of Harvard University Press, 1986.

European and American Imperialism

Christopher Hibbert, *The Great Mutiny: India 1857*. Harmondsworth, Middlesex, England: Penguin Books, 1978.

Lawrence James, *The Rise and Fall of the British Empire*. London: Abacus, 1994.

Jan Morris, *Farewell the Trumpets: An Imperial Retreat*. London: Penguin Books, 1978.

————, *Heaven's Command: An Imperial Progress*. London: Penguin Books, 1979.

————, *Pax Britannica: The Climax of an Empire*. London: Penguin Books, 1979.

Scott Nearing and Joseph Freeman, *Dollar Diplomacy*. New York: Modern Reader Paperbacks, 1969.

Samuel Peter Orth, *The Imperial Impulse: Background Studies of Belgium, England, France, Germany, Russia*. New York: Century, 1916.

Milton E. Osborne, *River Road to China: The Mekong River Expedition 1866–73*. New York: Liveright, 1975.

James C. Thomson Jr., Peter W. Stanley, and John Curtis Perry, *Sentimental Imperialists: The American Experience in East Asia*. New York: Harper Torchbooks, 1981.

East Asia

Edward R. Beauchamp and Akira Iriye, *Foreign Employees in Nineteenth Century Japan*. Boulder, CO: Westview Press, 1990.

Pearl S. Buck, *The Man Who Changed China: The Story of Sun Yat-sen*. New York: Random House, 1953.

Duong Van Mai Elliot, *The Sacred Willow: Four Generations in the Life of a Vietnamese Family*. New York: Oxford University Press, 1999.

John King Fairbank, *The Great Chinese Revolution: 1800–1985*. New York: Perennial/Harper and Row, 1986.

Akira Iriye, *Japan and the Wider World*. London: Longman, 1997.

Diana Preston, *The Boxer Rebellion*. New York: Walker, 1999.

Jonathan Spence, *God's Chinese Son: The Taiping Heavenly Kingdom of Hong Xiuquan*. New York: W.W. Norton, 1996.

Richard Storry, *A History of Modern Japan*. Baltimore: Penguin Books, 1960.

Suisheng Zhao, *Power Competition in East Asia*. New York: St. Martin's Press, 1997.

North America

Bruce Catton, *The Civil War*. New York: American Heritage Press, 1960.

Donald Barr Chidsey, *The California Gold Rush: An Informal History*. New York: Crown Publishers, 1968.

Bruce Collins, *The Origins of America's Civil War*. New York: Holmes and Meier, 1981.

Daniel Dawson, *The Mexican Adventure*. Freeport, NY: Books for Libraries Press, 1935.

Martin Luis Guzman, *The Eagle and the Serpent*. Trans. Harriet de Onis. Gloucester, MA: Peter Smith, 1969.

John M. Hart, *Revolutionary Mexico: The Coming and Process of the Mexican Revolution*. Los Angeles and Berkeley: University of California Press, 1997.

J.S. Holliday, *The World Rushed In: The California Gold Rush Experience*. New York: Simon and Schuster, 1981.

Brian Holden Reid, *The Origins of the American Civil War*. London: Longman Press, 1996.

Africa

Michael Attwell, *South Africa: Background to the Crisis*. London: Sidgwick and Jackson, 1986.

Anthony Nutting, *Scramble for Africa: From the Great Trek to the Boer War*. New York: Dutton, 1971.

Roland Oliver and J.D. Fage, *A Short History of Africa*. Harmondsworth, Middlesex, England: Penguin Books, 1962.

Science and Technology

Peter J. Bowler, *Charles Darwin: The Man and His Influence*. Oxford: Blackwell, 1990.

Arthur C. Clarke, *Voice Across the Sea*. New York: Harper and Brothers, 1958.

Stephen Jay Gould, *The Mismeasure of Man*. New York, W.W. Norton, 1981.

Ernest V. Heyn et al., *Fire of Genius: Inventors of the Past Century*. Garden City, NY: Anchor Press/Doubleday, 1976.

Banesh Hoffmann and Helen Dukas, *Albert Einstein: Creator and Rebel*. New York: Viking Press, 1972.

Arthur Knight, *The Liveliest Art: A Panoramic History of the Movies*. New York: Mentor/MacMillan, 1957.

Alan I. Marcus and Howard P. Segal, *Technology in America: A Brief History*. San Diego, CA: Harcourt Brace Jovanovich, 1989.

Marvin W. McFarland, "Wilbur and Orville Wright: Seventy-Five Years Later," in *The Wright Brothers, Heirs of Prometheus*. Ed. Richard P. Hallion. Washington, DC: Smithsonian Institution Press, 1978.

Martin V. Melosi, *Thomas A. Edison and the Modernization of America*. Glenview, IL: Scott, Foresman/Little, Brown Higher Education, 1990.

Walter Mih, *The Fascinating Life and Theory of Albert Einstein*. Huntington, NY: Korosha Books, 2000.

Hugh Joseph Schonfeld, *The Suez Canal in Peace and War 1869–1969*. Coral Gables, FL: University of Miami Press, 1969.

Holland Thompson, *The Age of Invention: A Chronicle of Mechanical Conquest*. New Haven, CT: Yale University Press, 1921.

Lynanne Wescott, *Wind and Sand: The Story of the Wright Brothers at Kitty Hawk*. Philadelphia: Eastern Acorn Press, 1985.

Arnold T. Wilson, *The Suez Canal: Its Past, Present, and Future*. London: Oxford University Press, 1933.

ABOUT THE EDITOR

Jeff Hay received a Ph.D. in history from the University of California, San Diego, where he taught in the innovative Making of the Modern World program. He now teaches world history at San Diego State University. In addition to editing two volumes of Greenhaven Press's Turning Points in World History series, Hay is working on a three-volume encyclopedia on the history of the Third Reich.